Modern Pistol Shooting

Modern Pistol Shooting

P. C. FREEMAN

FABER AND FABER
3 Queen Square
London

*First published in 1968
by Faber and Faber Limited
3 Queen Square London WC1
Reprinted 1968
Reprinted with minor corrections 1973
Printed in Great Britain by
Unwin Brothers Limited
The Gresham Press Old Woking Surrey England
All rights reserved*

ISBN 0 571 08503 2

© *1968 by P. C. Freeman*

Acknowledgements

It is impossible to write a book like this without the assistance of a great number of people. I would like to take this opportunity of thanking all who so willingly gave me helpful advice and criticism. In particular I would like to mention my wife, Peggy, for helpful discussion and patience whilst I have been engaged on this task; Colin Bennett, Nobby Clark and Charles Sexton, British Internationals and fellow members of the British Pistol Club, who have all examined the manuscript and contributed to the detail.

The Officer Commanding the United States Army Marksmanship Training Unit in Fort Benning, Georgia, has generously supplied material from their Training Manual and offers advice if readers are unable to find the solution to their problems. Karl Lanz, editor of the journal of the Union International de Tir, *Shooting Sport*, has kindly permitted me to use published material and P. Hediger of S. A. Hämmerli, Lensburg, Switzerland, has allowed me to use extracts from Hämmerli News and original photographs. A. J. Palmer, Esq., O.B.E., the Secretary of the National Smallbore Rifle Association, has agreed to the use of material published in the *Rifleman*, of which he is editor.

Finally I would like to thank Mr. G. W. Cafferata, Vice-Chairman of the National Smallbore Rifle Association and a member of the Pistol Technical Committee of the U.I.T., not only for writing the Foreword to this book but for the many years of leadership without which British Pistol Shooting would not have achieved its present status.

Contents

Foreword	page 15
Introduction	17
1. The First Step	19
2. Ranges and Range Discipline	27
3. Equipment	35
4. Stance and Grip	42
5. Aiming and Firing	50
6. Applying the Principles	58
7. Fault Analysis and Correction	73
8. Physical Condition	87
9. The Mental Approach	94
10. The Free Pistol	100
11. Rapid-Fire Shooting	116
12. Centre Fire	133
13. The Open Meeting	143
14. International Meetings	149
15. Coaching	163
Appendix A. Exercises	167
Appendix B. Organization of Pistol Shooting in Great Britain	172
Index	175

Illustrations

DIAGRAMS

Every shooter's ambition	page 18
1. Stance	43
2. Shape of gun stock	46
3. Model for demonstrating aim	51
4. Diagrammatic mechanism of single shot pistol	61
5. Diagrammatic mechanism of automatic pistol	62
6. Correction of elevation	66
7. Correction of direction	67
8. The aim	74
9. Vertically elongated group	76
10. Laterally elongated group	76
11. Incorrect sight picture showing strike of shot	77
12. Effect of deliberate errors in sighting	78
13. The effect of cant	79
14. Result of experiment to show effect of cant	80
15. Relation between parallel and angular errors	82
16. Sighting process when using mirror sights	105
17. Diagram showing optimum shooting conditions	110
18. Record card	114

ILLUSTRATIONS

PLATES

1. The International target used for 50 metres Free Pistol and 25 metres precision (C.F. & S.H.G.) *facing page* 32
2. The International Rapid Fire target used for Rapid Fire and Centre Fire Duelling at 25 metres — 32
3. A Pistol Gallery, N.R.A., Bisley — 32
4. Smith & Wesson Model 52; ·38 Special Semi-Automatic Pistol with very handsome engraving — 33
5. 'The Contender' by the Thompson Centre Arms, U.S.A. — 33
6. The Shooting Box opened and contents displayed — 48
7. Oblique Stance — 48
8. Oblique Stance (front view) — 48
9. 'In Line' Stance *after page* 48
10. Making sure that the stance is correct by lifting the arm — 48
11. (a) and (b). Correct Grip — 48
12. A grip made to exactly fit the hand by Wili Hofman — 48
13. Loading Single Shot Pistol (Webley) *facing page* 49
14. Cocking Single Shot Pistol (Webley) — 49
15. Author on aim. Shooting right-handed, but using left eye — 64
16. Author's son. Right-handed, using right eye — 64
17. The Aim, as seen by the eye — 65
18. Hämmerli CO_2 Pistol (·177 calibre) — 65
19. Free Pistol. A very easy natural stance — 96
20. Free Pistol Grip — 96
21. Free Pistol Grip — 96
22. Hämmerli Match Free Pistol — 97
23. Hämmerli Match Pistol fitted with mirror sights — 97

ILLUSTRATIONS

24.	Parabolic mirror foresight	*facing page*	112
25.	Front of rearsight		112
26.	Target as viewed through normal sights		112
27.	Target as viewed with mirror sights		112
28.	The Asaka range in Tokyo as used in the 1964 Olympic Games showing top screens or baffles and side screens	*after page*	112
29.	25 metre Rapid Fire Range in Cairo as used in the 1962 World Championships		112
30.	Hämmerli Rapid Fire Model 210		112
31.	Rapid Fire Grip (Hämmerli ·22 short Olympia)		112
32.	Opposite view of 31		112
33.	Rapid Fire Grip (top view)	*facing page*	113
34.	Tightening the grip by pulling back the skin so that slide will not foul the proud flesh		113
35.	Rapid Fire Stance: (1) Waiting for target to turn		128
36.	Opposite view of 35		128
37.	Rapid Fire Stance: (2) Target has turned		128
38.	Opposite view of 37	*after page*	128
39.	Rapid Fire Stance: (3) Shooting position		128
40.	Opposite view of 39		128
41.	Centre Fire—precision oblique stance		128
42.	·22 auto-loading pistol (Standard Hand Gun) (Hämmerli 208)		128
43.	A very simple hand-operated target for dry practice—Rapid Fire or Duelling		128
44.	Centre Fire—the revolver grip	*facing page*	129
45.	Centre Fire—taking the grip		129
46.	Centre Fire Duelling—waiting for target to turn		144
47.	Centre Fire Duelling—firing the shot		144
48.	Standard Hand Gun		145
49.	A target used for Centre Fire and Rapid Fire		145

Foreword

Pistol shooters who aspire to the attainment of a high standard of performance, or to the perfection of their existing techniques, will undoubtedly have searched the shelves of bookshops in vain in their attempts to find a really worthwhile book in English on modern pistol shooting. Unlike other forms of shooting, such as rifle shooting, both full-bore or small-bore, or sporting gun shooting, which are relatively well catered for, the sport of pistol shooting has been badly neglected by authors of shooting books. This is particularly so where International-style pistol shooting, as controlled by the Union International de Tir, is concerned. It is, of course, true that some very good books on modern pistol shooting, which adequately cover this particular aspect of the sport, have appeared in other countries, notably in the U.S.S.R. Undoubtedly the excellence of this literature has played a big part in bringing the U.S.S.R. to the forefront among pistol-shooting nations in recent years. Unfortunately, however, the books will remain unintelligible to the shooter who can only speak and understand the English language.

For this reason pistol shooters, handicapped by language problems, will welcome the present volume on pistol shooting, written by one of this country's best-known pistol shooters—Major P. C. Freeman, M.C., who has had a very successful shooting career during the past two decades.

Major Freeman started rifle shooting at a very early age, but it was not until 1949 that he took up pistol shooting. He quickly decided that if he was to become really proficient at this most

FOREWORD

difficult form of shooting, he would have to concentrate on it exclusively, and by doing this he quickly acquired a high degree of skill with the standard pistol and became British Pistol Champion in 1954. Since then he has contested the final stage of these Championships on four other occasions and has also shot for British teams in international matches in this country on eleven occasions. In addition to this, he has represented Great Britain in the European Championships at Milan in 1959 and at Bucharest in 1965 and in the World Championships at Wiesbaden in 1966.

His participation in championships organized by the Union International de Tir as a member of British teams, enables Major Freeman to write with authority in dealing with this aspect of competition shooting. For this reason they will be read with keen interest by all top-class pistol shooters who have ambitions to represent Great Britain in such championships in future years.

There is much in the book, too, of value to pistol shooters having more modest aspirations, whose ultimate ambitions may only be to represent their own club in one of the teams entered for competitions organized by their County or National Associations. The pistol shooting novice is also well catered for; so the book, as readers will soon discover for themselves, is one which will recommend itself to all students of the sport.

G. W. CAFFERATA

Introduction

'A man who is aiming high may be discouraged again and again when he realizes that he has not hit the mark. That discouragement is a much more hopeful sign than the self-complacency of another who aimed much lower and perhaps with more apparent success. In any case, to be satisfied with oneself is quite fatal.' This quotation is taken from *Day by Day*, the book of thoughts by the late Rev. W. H. Elliott and is the beginning of the thought for the 25th January, entitled 'Bull's Eye'.

The philosophy of life that is conveyed in these thoughts is quite applicable to the attitude of mind of the aspiring pistol shooter. I hope that in this book I have offered seeds of hope for the novice and food for thought for the expert.

I have laid down the basic principles and shown how the techniques have been developed from these principles, but I have not been dogmatic. I realize that techniques differ, and the technique that will suit one shooter may not suit another. If, therefore, there are statements with which the experts do not agree, I trust that they will not condemn them out of hand but will examine them to find the reasons for the differences.

Constructive criticism is one of the best means of improving the shooter's technique. The shooter should always be striving to improve his performance and will therefore be critical of his own efforts. I hope that my readers will find some answers to their problems and also points for discussion with their fellow shooters. I know that I have increased my own knowledge of the techniques whilst setting out the arguments and theories.

Every shooter's ambition

1

The First Step

The desire to shoot a pistol may have been aroused by talking to an enthusiast, by watching television or the cinema, or through a general interest in fire-arms. However the interest is aroused, the newcomer is presented with the problem of how to achieve the opportunity of actually firing a pistol.

All nations which regard shooting as a sport have national organizations which administer and control the sport. An approach to such an organization will enable the aspirant to be put in touch with his nearest club and then it is up to him to go along and make himself known. If the address of the national organization is not known, then inquiry should be made to the local police or a similar authority. In most countries the police control the licensing of fire-arms and often have jurisdiction over the clubs themselves. The local press quite often gives news of the activities of local clubs.

A visit to the local club will be the first step and the newcomer will find that he will be made welcome provided that he wishes to take an active interest in the recognized forms of shooting. If his interest is solely in combat or quick-draw shooting then he will need to find the clubs that specialize in this form. Such shooting is outside the scope of this book and is mainly restricted to those who need to be trained in such methods for service or law enforcement purposes.

Clubs vary considerably, but the majority are private in that the range is owned by the club and persons using the range must be members or guests of the club. In Great Britain, even the famous Bisley ranges are private as all persons using this range must either be individual members of the National Rifle Association or members of affiliated clubs. It is public to the extent that any such member may shoot on the range by paying the appropriate fee for the facilities required. Other countries have different conditions and there are many where the ranges are commercially owned and the public may shoot on payment. But such ranges will hardly enable the interested person to become a shooter unless facilities are available for him to learn or to be taught.

There are a number of countries where courses are organized for experienced shooters wishing to become instructors and where beginners can have proper instruction under such qualified instructors. For many an aspirant, however, these facilities are not available and he has to learn by picking up hints from fellow members who may not be much better than himself, or by learning from his own mistakes. If he is fortunate enough to live near a club with members in the top rank, then his progress will be much quicker. He should remember that the good shot also has his own shooting to do and may not have unlimited time available to help the beginner. What time he does have, he will gladly give.

Clubs vary from place to place and from indoor to outdoor. An outdoor range has the targets in the open and the shooters usually fire from a covered firing point. This can be a simple roof with a table under it or a far more elaborate structure properly heated, depending on the age and affluence of the club (and the enthusiasm of its members). Indoor ranges are completely enclosed and shooting is normally under artificial light. Some shooters find it difficult to change from an indoor to an outdoor range and vice versa, but if all indoor ranges were adequately illuminated from the firing point to the target, the change would be less apparent.

The majority of clubs are small and serve a small area or are restricted to a business or factory. They will be run by a small group of enthusiasts as a spare-time hobby. The club officials are to be respected and it is in the interest of all club members to see that their club officials have the support they need. There are no harder worked nor more maligned officials than the honorary secretaries of shooting clubs. However, the secretary is the official whom the prospective member should seek out to obtain all the information concerning the club—on what days and at what times it is open, what are the subscription rates, are club weapons available, what forms of pistol shooting are undertaken, are courses of instruction given, and so on. It is probable that the choice of club for a newcomer in any particular area is limited, as pistol clubs are not as common as rifle clubs, but he should be able to find one within a reasonable distance. Rifle clubs will frequently have pistol sections.

The potential member will not be allowed to join the club at once, but will be admitted as a probationary member for at least three months. This serves a dual purpose: the club officials can assess the newcomer to see if he is likely to become a keen and useful member of the club or one who does not maintain his interest; and on the other hand it enables the probationary member to see if the sport is to his liking and whether the club provides the amenities he requires. If the member understands this when he first applies to join, then he has no grievance if the probationary period is not followed by confirmed membership. The probationary membership principle is approved by police authorities as it enables the club secretary to confirm that the potential member has been accepted as a full member by the club. To enable shooters who have been admitted by a club as full members to own and carry fire-arms, they will be issued by the police with a fire-arms certificate which specifies the number and type of weapons and ammunition that may be acquired. It is in the interest of the sport that fire-arms certificates are not issued to unsuitable persons and club secretaries have the responsibility of giving proper references for their members when requested by the police authorities. The mere fact of joining a club should not be an automatic recommendation for the right to own and carry a fire-arm.

To enable the probationary member to learn the first principles, most clubs have their own weapons. These will be lent, for use on the club range, to members who do not own their own guns. They will usually be pistols equipped with factory grips or weapons given to the club by old members. They will probably

THE FIRST STEP

appear to be well used, but they will be in good condition and quite adequate for the trial period. Other members may lend their weapons from time to time but if they are adapted for use by the owner, it will be difficult for another shooter to use them. Using a club gun and borrowing other pistols on the range enables the newcomer to use a variety of weapons before deciding which one he will buy when he has received his fire-arms certificate.

The prospective member will probably wish to know the usual courses of fire. The majority of pistol shooting in Great Britain is with ·22 calibre and is deliberate shooting. The target is stationary and the shooter has enough time to deliberately aim and fire each shot. Besides being called deliberate, it is also known as 'slow fire'. The standard time for slow fire under N.S.R.A. rules is ten shots in ten minutes. Targets are shot at distances of up to 50 yards but the majority of ranges do not extend farther than 20 yards. Some ranges extend to 50 metres for Free Pistol shooting under U.I.T. rules.

The targets for deliberate shooting are square with a round black aiming mark. The remainder of the target is white, the paper used being preferably non-reflecting. This type of target is also used for timed and rapid fire, but with the scoring rings larger. The centre ring on the target usually scores ten points and each ring away from the centre has a value of one point less than the previous ring. There may be another dotted ring inside the centre ring, known as the 'X' ring; it is used in some competitions for deciding ties. Timed fire is five shots in twenty seconds and rapid fire is five shots in ten seconds. For this shooting, an automatic (self-loading) pistol is preferable, although revolvers can be used.

'Metric' targets are also used at various distances and these are proportionate to the 50-metre pistol target which has the size of aiming mark and scoring rings defined in the regulations of the U.I.T. This organization, the Union International de Tir or International Shooting Union, is a supra-national body which lays down and administers the rules governing the shooting competitions which are common to the majority of nations. This organization, on whose council the major shooting nations are

THE FIRST STEP

represented, also conducts World and Regional Championships and is largely responsible for the organization of the shooting events in the Olympic Games and similar events.

The standard 50-metre U.I.T. target is mainly used by advanced shooters with the free pistol at this range, but it is also the target for the standard pistol competition, the precision course at 25 metres for the centre-fire pistol and the women's standard handgun event. These targets can be scaled down for shorter distances.

A popular shoot, where the facilities exist, is 'silhouette', or rapid-fire shooting at figure-size targets at 25 metres. These targets are exposed for set intervals and one or more shots are fired at each exposure according to the competition. They are used in the U.I.T. rapid-fire pistol competition and also in the centre-fire and standard handgun duelling event. They, too, can be scaled down for shorter distances.

Competitions vary according to the requirements of the individual. To begin with there are rating competitions in which the entrant has to compete against a standard score to gain a rating or classification. There are individual competitions run by clubs, by counties and by national organizations. Competitors are placed in divisions according to their known standard. This can produce some surprising results, especially in the lower divisions, when a shooter may suddenly make a big improvement. The matches are shot on a postal basis, the shot targets being sent to an independent person for scoring. It is therefore very important that shooters study the rules concerning postal shooting and in particular those relating to witnessing. The whole basis of this procedure is mutual trust between shooters in ensuring the strict application of the rules wherever the shooting is done. The shooter must see that the person witnessing the shot is an officially accepted witness and the witness must see that the shooter has fired according to the rules for the competition. Severe action is taken against both shooter and witness if it is found that the rules have been contravened. It is to the credit of the sport that misdemeanours are few and far between.

The individual will also take part in local and national shoulder-to-shoulder competitions and championships. Here, too, he will

THE FIRST STEP

be shooting in his own class. He will find a friendly reception and will be able to watch the best shots in action, see other guns in use and discuss his problems with many people. He may find, however, that he will receive as many answers as he asks different people. By going to other ranges, he will see different types of competitions and shoot on a variety of ranges, giving him valuable experience.

Apart from individual competitions, clubs participate in leagues in which they enter one or more teams. The teams will be placed in divisions according to their declared average. The club secretary submits entries in which he nominates his teams and declares the team average. The main leagues will be run by the national association. The divisions will be made up of teams from all over the country and scores when published will show the individual names of the members comprising the club teams. If members have attended large meetings they will recognize the names of individuals of other teams and this adds interest to the competition. Matches are shot at regular intervals and dates for completion of each round will be published and stamped on the targets. If selected for a club team it should be a point of honour that the cards are fired in ample time in advance of the last date for shooting, and every effort should be made to make the best score possible. The club secretary or nominated official has to despatch the targets after they have been fired and witnessed and these targets have to be in the hands of the scorer by the given dates otherwise the scores will not be allowed.

Besides being affiliated to the national organization, clubs are also affiliated to regional or county associations as there are competitions based on such organizations which also have responsibilities under the national associations for local administration. There will be teams representing the county taking part in postal and shoulder-to-shoulder matches. To gain a place in such a team may seem a long way off for the beginner but he should be aware that these facilities exist and that shooting does not begin and end within his own club. The strength of county and national organizations depends wholly on the strength of the clubs and the interest of the members.

THE FIRST STEP

Beyond the county teams are the national teams competing in both international postal competitions and championship meetings. As in other sports it is a great honour to be selected for such teams and members are well aware that they are representing not only their nation but a great number of shooters who by providing competition have enabled the good shots to improve their techniques to international standards.

The way to the top can be a long process and owing to the very high standard required many never reach as far as the county teams, but all derive a great deal of pleasure from their shooting and the camaraderie of people from all walks of life competing on equal terms. It may be that one shooter can afford better equipment than another but that does not make him a better shot. Dedication combined with ambition is necessary to set the scores climbing in such a way that the newcomer can say that he is no longer a novice, the club member can say he is an expert and the expert may join the *élite*.

In Great Britain the N.S.R.A. have a national coaching scheme in which three national pistol coaches work under the direction of the chief national pistol coach. These coaches serve on the Council of the Association either as elected members or as invited observers. They are thus able to participate in the administration of the sport.

The country is divided by the Sports Council into regions for all sports and in each of these regions a regional pistol coach has been appointed. His function is to instruct county coaches within his region, to encourage the promising shooters and to ensure that the county coaches teach the club instructors. The aim of the scheme is to see that there is at least one qualified instructor in each club that includes pistol shooting in its programme. In this way a standard programme of basic training can be given to newcomers with a resulting benefit to all levels of the sport.

The national coaches are also responsible for training the National Squad for which the top shooters compete annually and from which the national teams are selected.

I.M.I. (Kynoch) Ltd have recently produced a film called 'Bang on Target' which shows some of the methods taught by club

THE FIRST STEP

instructors. This film can be borrowed from the I.M.I. film library.

Besides his interest in the practical aspect of shooting, the club member will find that there are other activities within the club, and a good club will have social activities. The club notice-board will not only give details of forthcoming matches and results of the previous ones but will be a mine of information of social and allied activities.

To keep interested members abreast of what is going on in the world of shooting, periodicals are published in many countries, national organizations include in their subscriptions the cost of their journal. The pistol shooter will find that these magazines will not be solely devoted to his particular side of the sport, but will include all aspects of shooting. Articles will all be of interest and will give a wider background to the sport of shooting as a whole.

Finally, and this is in the nature of a serious warning, a word about gun security. Guns should not be handled or displayed in clubrooms except in the part set aside for that purpose. This avoids the possibility of a mishap amongst people who may not be aware that a gun is being handled in the room. Keep guns in cases when not on the firing point and either put them in the gun room in a secure place or lock them in the boot of the car. Never leave guns lying about unattended—such carelessness asks for trouble, not only from the safety point of view but by putting temptation in the way of the unscrupulous. Shooters have a duty to their fellow sportsmen to let the general public see that they are responsible people. This attitude will mean that incidents involving fire-arms, which are always well publicized, will be seen in their proper perspective without detriment to the sport.

2

Ranges and Range Discipline

Ranges vary from the smallest club range with perhaps a couple of targets to the big international ranges where a hundred shooters can shoot at the same time. The construction of a range depends upon the need, the site and the money available.

Before a site can be developed, local authorities must consider the proposals in principle and in detail, and if satisfied that their requirements are met, will give their permission. Besides local authority approval, ranges also require police approval and safety certificates and the latter are usually granted by the military if the safety requirements are adequate. In the first place they require plans which must be approved by them before commencement, and then the range will be inspected on completion. Shooting cannot take place until range safety certificates have been issued. National associations will give advice on range construction and assist with the formalities. They may also be able to assist with grants and loans, which may sometimes be available from government funds.

Clubs should make very careful budgets when planning to allow for the unforeseen snags which will arise when actual construction commences. Most of the smaller ranges are built by the club members themselves and although at times enthusiasm may flag, the final result will be worth all the effort and time. The size and layout will depend on the needs of the club, the size of the site and the money available. It will of course save money if a disused quarry can be found on long lease, and more money can then be spent on amenities. If such a site cannot be found, then the amen-

RANGES AND RANGE DISCIPLINE

ities will have to wait. Details of construction will not be dealt with in this book but some guiding principles will be mentioned.

If the site will allow, the direction of the range should be such that the natural light comes from behind the firing point or as near to that as possible. The targets will then always be illuminated from the front and will never be in shadow, and the shooters will not be troubled with the sun coming into the front of the firing point.

The range should be level and cleared of all stones or other objects likely to cause ricochets. Target frames will be positioned so that no shooter will have to aim above his natural line of sight. There are many methods of fixing targets to frames, from thumb tacks to spring clips. Whatever method is adopted, ensure that the targets will remain in position in the worst conditions of rain and wind and that changing targets is quick and simple. Unless there is a protected danger area behind the targets in an arc where the bullets can fall harmlessly at their extreme range, stop butts will be required.

Stop butts will be built to the specifications laid down by the proper authority. The specification will define height and width according to the range and number of targets and the type of course that will be fired. The bullet stops must either be of soft earth or sand or will have metal plates deflecting the bullets downwards. They should be of a neutral colour to avoid glare. Any metal frames for targets should be timber faced to prevent deflection of bullets into safe areas.

The firing point should be covered to protect the shooters from sun, rain and wind and the cover should extend far enough in front of the point to protect the gun in the firing position and far enough behind to allow people to walk up and down without interfering with the shooter. Adjustable roof lights should be included in the roof. Partitions, either temporary or permanent, are desirable to give side protection.

The whole site should be grassed if possible to consolidate earthworks and to give a restful colour to the shooter's eyes, besides giving a pleasant appearance to the range. Baffles or screens can be built between the firing point and the targets to give

RANGES AND RANGE DISCIPLINE

further protection from wind and also to make the range safer by preventing high shots from going over the stop butt. This can also be prevented if there is a bar adjustable for height above the firing point to prevent the gun being lifted too high.

There must also be a clubhouse. This in the short term will be a simple hut where the members can take shelter when not on the firing point. For the long term the clubhouse will be as elaborate as funds will allow but it should envisage a clubroom, a gunroom, an office, a secure store, refreshment facilities and toilets.

The types of ranges briefly outlined are outdoor ranges which are preferable to indoor ones. Many clubs in towns and cities are unable to build outdoor ranges and have to use indoor ranges. Safety requirements are not usually as elaborate provided all the walls are bullet proof and adequate bullet catchers are provided at the butts. The lead from the bullets can be recovered at intervals from the stop butt, both indoor and outdoor, and can be sold to give a very useful source of income to the club. Earth or sand bullet stops should be periodically turned over to prevent hardening and so avoid a possible cause of ricochets. All metal surfaces must be faced with wood. Indoor ranges must be adequately lighted. Lighting should extend along the whole length of the range. It is a strain on the eyes if the targets are brilliantly lit whilst the rest of the range is in darkness. Attention should be paid to ventilation if the indoor range is totally enclosed.

The greater the amount of money available the more sophisticated can the range be made. The essential requirements are that whatever the conditions the shooter should be able to shoot in comfort. The firing point can be enclosed, with openings towards the targets, and proper heating, lighting and sound proofing installed. Target equipment which allows the shooter to remain on the firing point can be installed. This will either mean the building of a marker's gallery at the butts, which will need personnel to do the marking and target changing or the installation of travelling or stationary target apparatus which can be operated by the firer either manually or electrically. Such apparatus can be obtained commercially and is well advertised in international shooting journals.

RANGES AND RANGE DISCIPLINE

Rapid Fire/Duelling turning targets can either be made by the club members or obtained commercially. As this type of shooting is growing in popularity more of the smaller clubs are installing the equipment, often using ingenious forms of operation, mechanical, compressed air or electrical. The way will be found if there is the will! Such apparatus requires special safety precautions and specific authority to use it should be obtained.

On the assumption that a club is reasonably ambitious, it would be desirable to see a range constructed for precision shooting from distances of 10 yards (air pistol) to 50 metres (for free pistol) with any other specified intermediate distances being readily available and all being shot from the same firing point. If firing-point controlled target apparatus were installed then all or any distances could be used at the same time. Turning target apparatus at 25 metres should also be installed and the range constructed for use with small bore and centre fire. It should be stressed that range requirements for centre fire usually demand a higher safety standard than for small bore. On such a range it would be possible to fire all the courses in the national and international matches.

Besides safety requirements for the range itself there are other vital aspects of safety. THE HAND GUN IS A SHORT-BARRELLED WEAPON WHICH CAN BE QUICKLY POINTED IN ANY DIRECTION. This may sound a very obvious statement but it is vitally important and one of the many points to be remembered both by the individual and by range officials when considering the safety of the individual. It is therefore imperative that a rigid set of rules be laid down for pistol shooters, both on and off the range. The principles that must be adhered to are:

(1) Always assume a weapon is loaded until positively proved otherwise.

(2) Always when handling a weapon point it down the range or in a safe direction.

(3) Always be sure of your target before touching the trigger.

(4) Always have the weapon in a secure place when not on the firing line.

RANGES AND RANGE DISCIPLINE

These points will now be amplified both as regards the individual and the official responsible for the conduct of shooting.

As has already been stated the pistol is a short-barrelled weapon and can easily be pointed in any direction. It is therefore of paramount importance that very great care is taken when handling such weapons. *When first picking up a gun make sure that it is unloaded.* With a single-shot weapon the chamber or breech can be easily inspected; with a revolver the chamber can be revolved to see that it is empty; and with an automatic the magazine is first removed and then the slide pulled back to see that there is no cartridge in the chamber. This must be done whether the weapon is being handled by the shooter OR IS BEING HANDED TO SOMEONE ELSE FOR INSPECTION. The shooter should not only examine his own weapon but also see that the recipient inspects it. NEVER TAKE ANOTHER PERSON'S WORD THAT A WEAPON IS CLEAR.

When handling or giving a weapon to another person see that the barrel is pointing in a safe direction. The gun must NEVER be pointed at another person or handled with the hand over the end of the barrel. The only direction to point a weapon is down the range or at the floor of the gun room. It should be a point of honour amongst shooters to see that children are taught when playing with toy guns never to point them at other people.

Be sure that when the shooter does point a loaded weapon on the range that it is pointed at the proper target and only then when permission has been given because the range is clear.

When not on the firing line the weapon should be put away in the gun case and not left lying about. It is so easy to pick up and look at a gun that is lying on a table, especially if it is an unusual or a new type. It is the responsibility of the shooter, as soon as he has finished his shoot, and before he has left the firing point, to inspect his gun to see that it is empty and then to put it away. It might be that his case is behind the point or in the clubhouse. In this situation the gun must be made safe and carried open, if a single-shot then with the breech open, if a revolver with the chamber exposed and if an automatic with the magazine removed and the slide held back.

These principles do not prevent enthusiasts from inspecting

other people's weapons and discussing points of detail. This must not be done on the firing point but in a place set aside for the purpose on the range or in the gun room in the clubhouse and only when all interested parties have made quite sure that the gun is safe. It must be stressed here that on no account should any attempt be made to inspect an unfamiliar weapon without having the proper procedure demonstrated and explained by a competent person.

Guns must never be touched without the owner's express permission even though the gun may be a familiar model. They should never be loaded unless on the firing point and then only when permission has been given by the range officer. Guns should never be snapped on an empty chamber when inspecting a weapon. This can cause damage to the firing pin.

Guns at home must be kept in a secure place under lock and ammunition should be kept locked in a separate place of security. Children should not be permitted to handle 'real' fire-arms until they are old enough to be correctly instructed and fully understand the dangers.

It is fair to state that there are no 'accidents' with fire-arms. Such 'accidents' as do occur are caused by careless and negligent disregard of the cardinal principles of safety.

A considerable responsibility is placed on the officials in charge of ranges to see that the safety rules are observed. It must be made clear to shooters on the firing line that there is only one person in charge and that his word is law. In the first place he should ensure that there are no people in the area of the range who might be in a position of danger, and shooters must not take their place on the firing point until this has been done. They should not handle their guns until permission has been given. Weapons must be kept safe on the firing-point bench until the range officer has given the order to load and no weapon may be handled whilst people are in front of the firing point, for instance during target changing. The range officer will see that the range is clear before giving the shooters permission to handle their weapons or to load. Firing must not commence until the order is given and shooters must IMMEDIATELY cease fire when so ordered.

1. (*left*) The International target used for 50 metres Free Pistol and 25 metres precision (CF & SHG). The score is 49/50.
2. (*right*) The International Rapid Fire Target used for Rapid Fire and Centre Fire Duelling at 25 metres.

3. A Pistol Gallery. N.R.A., Bisley.

4. Smith & Wesson Model 52. ·38 Special Semi-Automatic Pistol with very handsome engraving. (*Springfield Arms Co. Ltd.*)

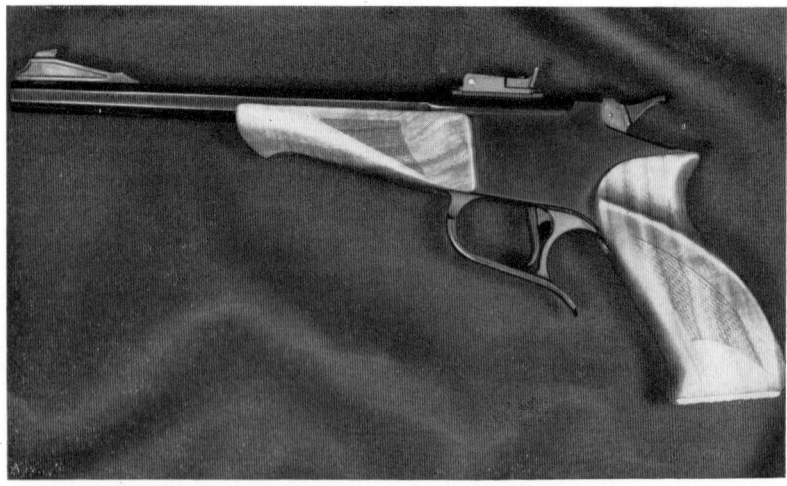

5. 'The Contender' by the Thompson Center Arms, U.S.A. A single shot pistol with interchangeable barrels for either rim or centre fire cartridge in various calibres. (*Springfield Arms Co. Ltd.*)

RANGES AND RANGE DISCIPLINE

In their own interests shooters must comply with the range officer's instructions as a safety precaution. It may be that the order to cease fire during a shoot may inconvenience some people, but safety is always the overriding factor and range officers must not hesitate to stop shooting if they think that is the right thing to do at the time. In competitions a re-shoot or extended time can always be given, but no amount of time can undo an injury. The range officer, after giving the order 'cease fire', whether in an emergency or not, will then order 'unload' and every shooter must see that this is done and on request show his gun to the range officer keeping the barrel pointed down the range. Before anybody is allowed forward from the firing point all weapons must be checked by the range officer and laid on the bench in a safe condition. Guns must on no account be touched until the range officer gives the appropriate order.

In the case of a malfunction or breakage of a weapon during a Timed competition the weapon must be laid on the firing point with the barrel pointing up the range and the range officer informed at once. He will have the pistol examined at the end of the shoot and if satisfied that the fault can be rectified will allow extension of time. On no account should the shooter attempt to rectify the fault during the shoot as this might cause an accident and will also render the shooter liable to disqualification.

It should be a matter of principle that range safety regulations are posted in the range in a prominent place. Range officers and club officials should know the telephone number of the local emergency services in case of need. It is very advisable to have first-aid equipment on hand not only for emergencies, but for the casual injury that can occur anywhere.

Range officers will be appointed for organized shooting, but in ordinary club shooting members using the range will be responsible for range and personal safety. An experienced member will be delegated to take charge. The range safety aspect of international meetings will be dealt with in the appropriate chapter.

Ranges should be kept tidy and empty cartridge cases placed in containers. Empty cases can be sold, but before being bagged for despatch to scrap metal merchants, or return to ordnance, they

RANGES AND RANGE DISCIPLINE

must be carefully inspected to see that no live rounds are included. A certificate to this effect must be given. Besides making the range untidy, cartridge cases on the floor are uncomfortable and can be dangerous when trodden on, and make the finding of dropped live rounds very difficult. Empty cartridge boxes and used targets should be placed in the bin and disposed of at frequent intervals. Notices on the range should be clearly displayed and obsolete ones removed.

It is relevant at this point to add a further note on safety. Not only should the shooter and the range officials be thoroughly acquainted with and practice safety regulations but they must see that weapons with inherent faults are not used. It is no good following the other rules correctly if the gun does not come up to standard. It is the responsibility of the shooter to see that his gun is in good repair and not to tinker with it unless he is absolutely sure of his actions. Weapons can be damaged accidentally and become unsafe, so safety mechanisms should be frequently tested. Trigger actions should not be so fine that the bearing surfaces will not hold when under tension, and incorrect size and load of ammunition must be avoided.

This book is written for the responsible shooter and all readers should see that their fellow shooters adopt a responsible attitude to safety. Set a good example and do not tolerate irresponsible behaviour—there is no latitude for error.

3

Equipment

The first item on a pistol shooter's list of equipment will, of course, be a pistol or pistols and there is endless discussion on which are the most suitable weapons. It is not proposed in this book to discuss the advantages and disadvantages of any particular make of pistol as this would be a volume on its own. It is necessary to discuss broadly the types of weapon that are generally used. The individual will take advice when he comes to buy his pistol as models change quite frequently and he will need the best gun he can afford for the kind of shooting he wishes to take part in.

Slow fire or deliberate shooting can be fired with a single-shot pistol and if the shooter wishes to restrict his shooting to this, then he will find that the single shot is the best gun. The single shot has to be reloaded for each shot and this fact alone makes the shooter take a break between each shot. He will have time to consider the result of the previous shot and make his plan for the following shot. The single-shot pistol is a simple pistol with very few moving parts. It is also the cheapest pistol on the market, and will shoot very high scores in the hands of an expert. The Free pistol for 50-metre shooting is one of the most expensive but is an essential when competing in the top classes.

If the shooter wishes to participate in shooting where there is insufficient time to reload between shots then he will have to acquire a revolver or an auto-loading pistol. These are often referred to as 'automatic' pistols but this is a misnomer. Automatic pistols will continue firing whilst the trigger remains

EQUIPMENT

pressed. Auto-loading pistols will only fire one shot each time the trigger is pressed but will automatically reload after the shot is fired. Fully automatic pistols would be a handicap to the shooter. A good auto-loading pistol will be just as accurate as a single shot and can be used equally well in the deliberate courses of fire; ·22 revolvers, either purpose made or converted, are seldom used by top-ranking shooters for serious target shooting.

Centre-fire pistols are either revolvers or auto-loading. There are a few single-shot models for target shooting as there are very few competitions which involve deliberate shooting only. Most competitions in this category also involve rapid fire and often it is obligatory to use the same pistol for both courses as in the U.I.T. C/F event. Most centre-fire shooting is for calibres of ·32 to ·38 but there is still some shooting in calibre of ·45, mainly in the United States. The target-model quality revolver in ·38 calibre maintains its popularity amongst the top class of shooter.

Every country which has an armament industry will produce pistols of various types and calibres. Many are not suitable for target shooting and the advice of a reputable gunsmith or experienced shooter should be taken before buying a new gun. Advice will never be lacking but if the shooter knows the type of weapon he wants and how much he can afford, then he can narrow the choice. It is often possible to buy weapons secondhand, but this should only be considered when the seller is known or recommended. It is possible to have pistols on trial. When a new pistol is being bought, inquiry should be made of the service and spare parts availability as this may decide the choice of weapon. At all times make sure that the seller has authority to sell and the buyer authority to buy. Illegal weapons are not only a source of embarrassment but can involve the holder in criminal proceedings.

In considering the maintenance of pistols, it must be remembered that pistols are subjected to some pretty rough treatment. Every time that they are fired a force of about 4 tons is developed in the chamber and on the breech face at the same time. Corrosive products are produced from the result of the combustion of the propellant; these are partly countered by the use of self-lubricating bullets. Guns are constantly handled and moisture from the skin will cause surface corrosion if the weapon is not properly looked after.

Guns will always have a resale value and this will be higher if the shooter maintains the weapon in a good condition. The external appearance of the gun will repay frequent cleaning and when not in use it should be kept in a clean oil-impregnated cloth in a dry place. The mechanism should be kept free from the grease accumulating from the cartridge lubricant. This grease will build up after a time and will trap grit and fouling which will abrase and corrode the metal surfaces in the mechanism. It is neither a difficult, nor a specialist, task to keep a gun clean and to see that the barrel does not become fouled. Modern ammunition is self-lubricating and anti-corrosive and barrels do not need cleaning too often. This does not mean that they should be neglected and an occasional clean does not come amiss. It is wise to clean before an important match and then to fire a number of rounds through the barrel before commencing the shoot. When a barrel is cleaned, it should be first brushed out with an oiled brush from the breech end. If the cleaning rod is inserted from the muzzle end, damage can occur to the end of the barrel at the vital point where the bullet leaves the barrel. After oiling to loosen the fouling and grease, the barrel should be wiped out with flannelette a number of times until the cloth comes through clean. Flannelette patches of the correct size can be obtained from any gunsmith. The cloth should be wound round the jag leaving a free end nearest to the handle. The rod is then inserted into the barrel from the breech end and pushed up and down several times with a smooth motion, making sure that the cloth remains completely covering the jag. When the barrel is clean and it is not intended to use it at once it should be lightly oiled. *Before firing the oil must be wiped out* or a ring bulge, ruining the barrel, can occur. A new gun will possibly be preserved with grease and all this must be removed before attempting to fire the pistol.

If after removing superficial fouling the barrel still appears to be dirty, a well-oiled soft bronze brush should be used to remove the deposit. This is usually lead stripped from the bullets and can

EQUIPMENT

be caused by imperfection in the surface of the barrel. A good barrel will last a lifetime if it is looked after.

The mechanism can be cleaned with white spirit and very lightly oiled, unless the manufacturer suggests other methods, and then it is wise to follow his instructions. When dismantling the mechanism, the instructions issued with the gun must be followed. It is seldom necessary to use any force, only care with the proper tools. It will be wise to let an experienced shot dismantle a new gun so that the new owner can see what should be done. It is very unwise to tamper with the mechanism of a gun unless the shooter has the experience and knowledge. The pistol is a dangerous weapon and tampering with the mechanism without knowledge could result in an unsafe gun. This particularly applies when adjustments are being made to the trigger. There are adequate gunsmiths available, both professional and amateur, and they should be consulted in case of the slightest doubt. Alterations to other parts of the gun, i.e. sights or stock, can be safely undertaken.

The pistol will be no use without ammunition. There are many brands of ·22 and centre-fire ammunition and most are suitable in pistols, except high-velocity and hollow-nose sporting ammunition. Ammunition is made specially for pistols and it is recommended that well-tried ammunition is used. Rapid-fire pistols can be chambered for ·22 'short'. This ammunition carries a smaller load than 'long rifle' and is widely used by shooters up to 25 metres. It is quite accurate at this range but is not recommended at longer ranges. Ammunition is sold in boxes containing 50 rounds and is obtained on the range. Unless the shooter has the authority to possess ammunition, he must not take any away from the range.

Factory-made centre-fire ammunition is expensive. The best match ammunition is known as 'wad cutter'. This has a flat nose and cuts a very clean hole in the target, giving very little room for argument on the value of the shot. Service ammunition is round nosed and jacketed and this makes rather a small and ragged hole in the target. There is, however, a growing interest in hand load-

EQUIPMENT

ing. This is very much cheaper than commercial ammunition, though in some countries factory reloads can be obtained in part exchange for empty cases. If the shooter has the time then he can undertake his own hand loading. This must be done very carefully and with the proper equipment. It is a dangerous task unless all precautions are taken, and if the loader is impatient then he may make very dangerous ammunition. This will not only be a hazard to himself but to the innocent bystander. All parts that make the complete cartridge must be examined before they are assembled. Care must be taken when casting the lead bullets to avoid lead poisoning. This is not to be confused with lead poisoning from the wrong end of a gun, but comes from lead absorbed into the system from fumes and constantly handling lead. Adequate ventilation when smelting and a good scrub up when lead has been handled will give the safeguards needed. If the hand loader suffers from headaches and lethargy after such work he should consult a doctor.

Accidents have occurred from faulty ammunition, and not always hand-loaded ammunition. Many major mishaps have been due to incorrect ammunition being used in the gun. This will be either ammunition which does not properly fit or overloaded ammunition; both can blow a gun apart and cause serious injury. Too light a load may be insufficient to expel the bullet from the barrel, and if this is not noticed at once and another round is fired, the least it will do is to bulge the barrel, and at worst it will burst it.

There are many accessories used by shooters and he should keep them in a tailor-made box. Pistol boxes can be bought but the majority of shooters make their own. Some use a simple hold-all while others build themselves elaborate cases holding all their guns which when opened out become a fixture for the telescope. Before any shooter decides to make his own he should have a good look at others and then plan for his own requirements taking the best points of others into his own design. Some are beautifully finished, often embellished with badges.

The guns should fit into the box so that they will not move during transport and remain protected from other metal objects in the box. They can either be held by cloth-covered clips, laid

EQUIPMENT

in soft plastic cut to shape or wood covered with baize. Some shooters prefer to carry their pistols in sheepskin-lined cases which not only protect the guns from damage but keep the external parts of the gun from rusting.

After his gun, the most important item of equipment the shooter will need will be a telescope. This will be used for spotting the position of the shot holes in the target, besides checking that the target is the right one! There are many types of telescopes in a wide range of prices. The most suitable one will be of sufficient magnification to see shot holes clearly at 50 metres, small enough to fit into the shooting box, not too heavy in weight but robust enough to stand frequent handling. With the telescope, the shooter needs a stand to support it as near as possible at eye level. Some shooters have a clamp on their shooting box, others clamp a stand to the bench or use a free-standing tripod stand. The telescope needs maintenance from time to time.

The shooter will keep in his box other smaller items, such as tools which he may need to adjust the sights or dismantle his gun in an emergency—screwdrivers and punches. There will be a space for ammunition and a block for holding the cartridges in use. He should carry such spare parts as may be needed in an emergency, these are best put in a small tin with a tight-fitting lid and a drop of oil put into the tin. He may also carry a very fine stone and a fine file. He will also include cleaning equipment, rod, jag, brushes, flannelette, and cleaning and lubricating oils.

If the shooter is shooting out of doors he will need a long peaked cap to shield his eyes. The underside of the peak should be of a non-reflecting material and either grey or green in colour. Some shooters also fit side flaps to the peak to restrict sideways vision and thereby assist concentration.

Besides wearing caps, shooters will be seen with ear protectors. There are two main kinds, ear plugs, which fit into the ear and filter off the high intensity sounds that cause damage, and ear muffs which fit over the ears and prevent excessive noise from reaching the ears. Either type gives proper protection and also assist the shooter in concentration. It is important that they are used as continual exposure to high-intensity noise will cause deaf-

EQUIPMENT

ness. It is just as important for spectators to use them. Both types can be obtained from any reputable gun dealer.

Pistol shooters are permitted to use orthoptics but lenses fitted to the guns are not permitted. The orthoptic can either be an adjustable iris fitted to spectacles with a suction cup or more elaborate shooting spectacles. If the shooter has defective vision he is allowed such lenses as will correct his vision and also coloured lenses to improve the clarity of vision and filter off the dazzle from strong sunlight. Special shooting glasses have frames which can be adjusted for angle and height so that the centre of the lens will be in front of the eye in the aiming position. A black or transluscent disc or occluder can be fixed in front of the non-aiming eye, allowing peripheral vision.

The shooter should provide himself with means for blacking his sights. Although sights are dark in colour they will still reflect light and this will be apparent when aiming. They should be dulled by the addition of a thin coating of carbon to a flat black appearance. This 'black' may come out of a bottle as a suspension of carbon in spirit but it is difficult to obtain a really smooth matt surface by this method. Most shooters prefer to make their own soot on the spot using a candle, camphor or an oily rag and hold the sights in the sooty part of the flame. The soot will deposit on the cooler surface of the sight. A popular and probably the best method is to use a small acetylene lamp which can be bought at any gun shop. A box of matches or cigarette lighter will have to be carried and in an emergency will themselves give good results.

A score book will be found in the shooter's box. This can be detailed showing diagrams for the position of each shot or just a record of the scores. If properly kept, this will help the shooter to analyse his shooting and pinpoint consistent errors. Score books can either be purchased or home made.

Other odd items find their way into the pistol box, such as a cloth for wiping the hands, sweets and a magnifying glass. The box should be kept secure and, if possible, fitted with a lock or padlock. In spite of all the equipment mentioned above, the shooting box will be of a reasonable size and easily carried by means of a handle or shoulder strap.

4

Stance and Grip

This chapter will discuss in detail the principle involved in taking up the correct position and gripping the gun before considering the aiming and firing. There will be slight differences depending on the type of weapon used and the course of fire and any differences will be dealt with in the chapters concerned. The differences are in detail and not in fundamental principle.

Before a shot can be fired the firer must be standing properly balanced and on a firm base, these together are spoken of as the stance. The object of the stance is to ensure that when the aim is taken the pistol is in line with the target without the shooter having to make any conscious effort to align the pistol other than to raise his arm. This fundamental principle applies to all forms of sport and a good result cannot be expected if the sportsman is off balance. The golfer places his feet so that he will get a natural swing of the club; the footballer will be perfectly balanced on one leg whilst he accurately kicks the ball with the right amount of force in the right direction with the other foot.

In pistol shooting there are basically two schools of thought on the position of the body and both give good balance. There is the oblique stance in which the line across the feet is at an angle of about 45 degrees to the line of fire, and the stance where the feet are along the line of fire. A study of shooters at an international meeting gives the impression that in deliberate shooting the majority prefer the latter stance.

In either stance the heels are about 18 inches apart with the toes turned slightly out so that the shooter feels that he is well

STANCE AND GRIP

balanced. It is taken for granted that the shooter will be standing on a level surface. If shooting outdoors on an uneven firing point the shooter will have to move around until he feels that the ground is firm and level under his feet.

It will be necessary for the shooter to shuffle about until he feels comfortable. After a time it becomes habit to take up the correct

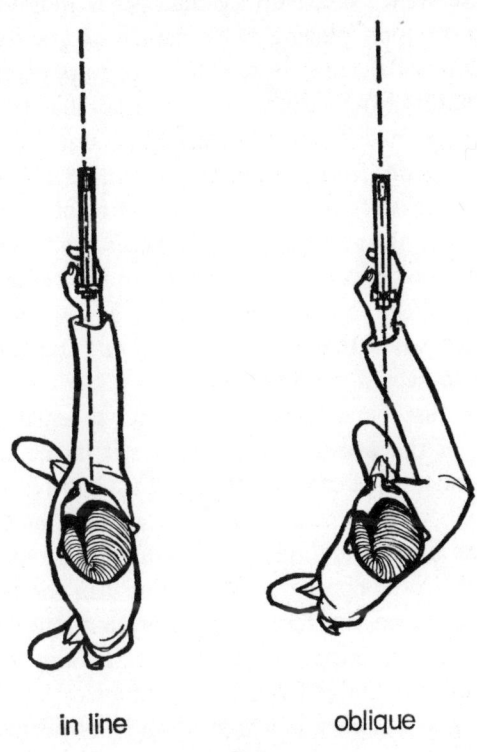

in line   oblique

1. *Stance*

position and the shooter can leave the range and on his return take up the same position without difficulty. At the start it will take longer to find the right stance and the novice will remain in the same position throughout a series of shots. Some, having found the right position, outline the position of their feet with chalk.

It is important that the shooter is comfortable about the feet. He should wear the same type of footwear whenever he shoots so

STANCE AND GRIP

that the feel of the stance is the same. It is preferable to wear a light boot to give support to the ankle, as the thrust of the body weight in an open stance tends to be borne on the outside of the foot. It is also important that good socks are worn to keep the feet comfortable. Any small thing that will make the shooter feel comfortable should be used.

The precise stance taken up by the firer is individual and in theory depends upon placing one's centre of gravity vertically above the centre of the area in which the feet are placed in order to ensure stability. It must be remembered that the centre of gravity will be in a different position when standing erect with the arms by the sides from the position it will be in when holding the gun in the outstretched hand. The centre of gravity will be displaced towards the gun and it will be necessary by body adjustment to bring the centre of gravity back to the centre line. It is by adjustment of the feet that this is done, as there should be no muscular strain when the arm is raised. Some shooters will lean back slightly to keep a good balance.

The head must be in an erect position to ensure the most effective use of the eyesight and because it is the natural and relaxed position of the head. People are of such different sizes and shapes that nobody, however expert, can lay down an exact stance that will apply universally. The final adjustment must be individual and made in the aiming position. The arm should be raised holding the gun and the feet shuffled around until the arm is roughly naturally pointing at the target. It may be that the natural position so obtained will be asymmetrical. This does not matter so long as stability is achieved and the position is comfortable.

The unengaged hand and arm is not to be forgotten. The arm should not be allowed to hang free but should be put into a pocket or hooked into the belt. If a proper shooting jacket is used it should have pockets cut diagonally so that the hand fits easily into the pocket at the right angle. Some shooters also like to hold something, such as a soft rubber ball. The arm used in this way improves the stability of the body. A free hand during firing is a nuisance and a distraction.

STANCE AND GRIP

Having secured a comfortable stance it is now necessary to check that the position is correct in relation to the line of sight. The details of correct grip and aim will be given later but at this point it is assumed that they are being taken correctly. Gripping the pistol in the extended arm, with the forearm straight and the elbow locked, but not strained, take an aim on the target. Then lower the pistol and close the eyes. Raise the pistol again, with the eyes closed and when the shooter thinks the pistol is on aim, open the eyes and at that instant see where the pistol is pointing in relation to the target. The vertical aspect of the aim is not important, only the lateral. If the stance is correct then the pistol will be pointing at a line vertically through the centre of the target. If it is pointing to one side or the other then the stance has to be moved. If the gun is to the right then the position has to be pivoted to the left. The trial aims will be repeated and the feet shuffled about until the natural aim is correct. It must be borne in mind that the whole position must be moved to maintain the natural balance. The object of obtaining a natural aim is to avoid strain on the muscles which align the pistol. Such strain would undoubtedly induce errors, especially towards the end of a long shoot. The shots will tend to follow the line of natural aim when the muscles are relaxed or tired.

Before an aim can be taken, the shooter must grip the pistol correctly. The manufacture of grips would almost fill a book by itself and shooters spend long hours talking about them and making them. The majority of factory grips are not really suitable for target shooting unless the competition rules expressly forbid their alteration. No two shooters have exactly the same shape of hand and therefore it is impossible for factory grips to fit more than a few individuals. There are gun dealers and commercial firms which make grips to fit the shooter but most like either to make their own or adjust the grips as supplied with the pistol. The essential elements of the grip are that it shall be almost impossible to grip it in more than one way and that when the pistol is raised and aimed, it will be pointed at the correct place on the target, always assuming that the firer has taken up the correct stance. Such a definition of a good grip may sound simple

STANCE AND GRIP

but any shooter will say that the making of a good pair of grips is a very difficult task. Many grips are made almost right and then the shooter persists with these for fear of an incorrect adjustment.

The grip must be shaped so that the natural 'V' between the forefinger and thumb is intersected by the line of the barrel. The hand should fit comfortably round the grip so that, with the exception of the forefinger, all parts of the hand are in contact

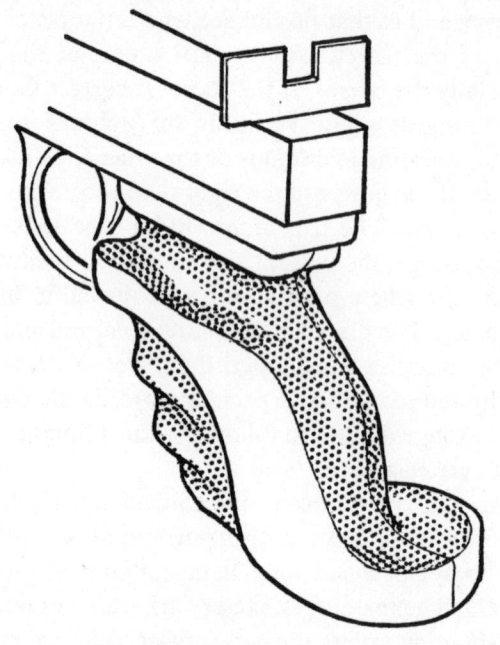

2. Shape of gun stock

The shaded part of the grip is critical. This must be fitted to the shooter's hand and the angle of slope determines the angle of the gun in relation to the line of sight.

with the grip and the underside of the frame rests naturally on the middle finger. The hold should be firm but not tight. Too tight a hold will mean tense muscles and induce tremor into the pistol from the pulse. Too loose a hold will not enable the firer to maintain a steady aim or trigger pressure. Some shooters hold to the theory that the hand should only come into contact with the grip where this is essential. The points of contact are the palm rest, the top shelf on the palm side of the grip and the underside of the frame where the weight of the pistol is taken on the middle finger. The theory is based on the supposition that the smaller the area of the hand in contact with the grip, the greater will be the positive feel and the better, therefore, the control. It is also put forward to support this theory that the part of the hand not in contact with the pistol cannot communicate spontaneous muscle movements (twitches) to the pistol. The general consensus of opinion is against this theory although it can give very good results for the individual shooter.

Through the grip the weight of the pistol is transferred to and held by the hand. This weight transfer must be even, part of it is taken through the gentle firmness by which the grip is held and part by that portion of the hand and fingers on which the grip rests. The fingers should pull back the grip into the ball of the thumb and the pressure exerted in line with the axis of the pistol. The main rear pressure will be exerted by the second and third fingers and the little finger will rest on the platform at the bottom of the grip, in order to maintain the position of the grip. The fingers should be close together but not pinched. Although a thumb rest is usually built into the grip no pressure must be exerted by the thumb which plays a similar role to the little finger in positioning the hand on the grip. Any pressure from the thumb will push the pistol downwards and to the right. The forefinger should be held free from the grip. The pad of this finger should fall onto the lower part of the trigger and pressure will then be applied directly to the rear.

The grip can be made to extend over the back of the hand but it is recommended that this should only be partial and not close fitting. Undue pressure on the back of the hand will compress the whole hand and make the muscles act as a compressed spring. This may produce a poor shot which defies fault analysis. Some shooters have a rigid strap at the back of the grip of their rapid fire pistols which helps to position the grip within the hand, but does not compress the hand.

The grip can be made to extend backwards over the back of the

STANCE AND GRIP

hand either completely or partially. This enables some of the weight to be taken by additional surface and also helps to give a firm grip if this extension is made close fitting. The extension can also cover the notch between the forefinger and thumb and this determines the upward limit of the position of the hand within the grip. Care must be taken when making these extensions to allow the forefinger free movement. The bottom of the side of the hand can be supported and this support will go round the front of the grip to support the little finger. The extension over the back of the hand is an upwards continuation of the palm rest.

It must be borne in mind that regulations are laid down which define the maximum size of grips for certain competitions. This can be overcome by making more than one pair of grips if it is necessary to use the same gun in differing competitions. It only takes a few minutes to change grips. Whatever type of grip is made or used, it must not extend to include the wrist joint. The wrist must be quite flexible. It is forbidden to wear any aid to support the wrist; even a watch strap could cause disqualification.

The construction of the grip will vary from person to person. Most shooters start with the original grip and adjust it by removing surplus wood and adding plastic wood where necessary until the required shape is reached. Plastic wood can be built on in layers and pressed into position whilst holding the pistol in the proper position. The hand is then gently removed and the plastic wood allowed to dry. Rough surfaces are then smoothed with glass paper and the pistol is then gripped again to see if any additional material is required or if surplus has to be removed. This process can go on for some time until the shooter is satisfied that he has made a good fit. The balance of the pistol is important and too much weight must not be put on the back of the pistol or the centre of gravity will be moved too far back. The weight of the pistol must be felt to give it stability. Lightweight materials, such as balsa wood, can be used in grips provided they are filled or laminated. Some shooters even bring tools on the range and make adjustments between shots trying to get the perfect grip!

If the shooter finds that he is making a good grip in this way, he may venture into making the grips completely from scratch.

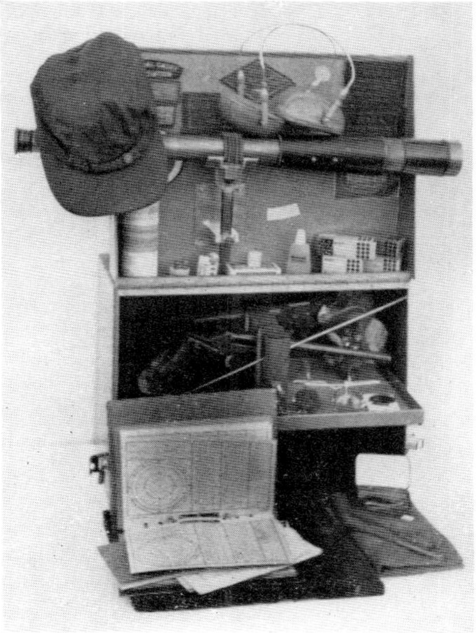

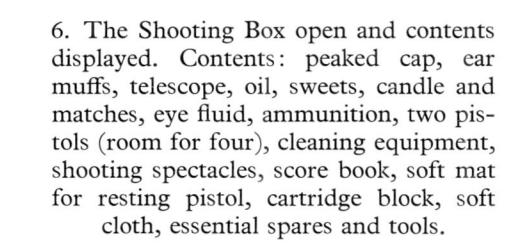

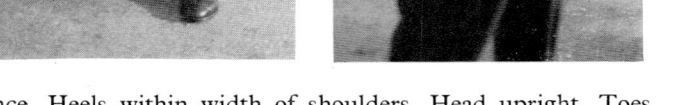

6. The Shooting Box open and contents displayed. Contents: peaked cap, ear muffs, telescope, oil, sweets, candle and matches, eye fluid, ammunition, two pistols (room for four), cleaning equipment, shooting spectacles, score book, soft mat for resting pistol, cartridge block, soft cloth, essential spares and tools.

7. (*left*) Oblique Stance. Heels within width of shoulders. Head upright. Toes pointed slightly outwards. Left hand supported. Also shows lift of arm and angle of wrist to bring sights to eye level. (C. H. Sexton)

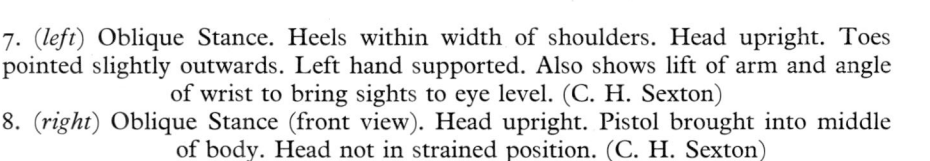

8. (*right*) Oblique Stance (front view). Head upright. Pistol brought into middle of body. Head not in strained position. (C. H. Sexton)

9. 'In Line' stance. (B. Girling)

10. Making sure that the stance is correct by lifting the arm. (Author's wife in centre.)

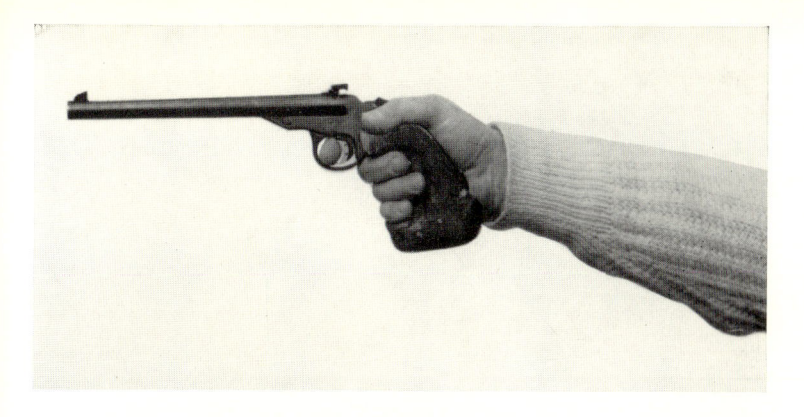

11 (a) and (b). Correct grip—seen from both sides. Fingers well supported. First pad of trigger finger on trigger.

12. A grip designed and made by Wili Hofman to the exact dimension of the hand.

13. Loading Single Shot Pistol (Webley). Note: All manipulation with the left hand as the right hand has already been positioned correctly in the grip. Trigger finger clear of trigger.

14. Cocking Single Shot Pistol (Webley). Right hand in correct grip, finger off the trigger, manipulation with left hand.

STANCE AND GRIP

Rough stocks are usually available for all makes of pistol, or the shooter can fit his own wood to the gun. Circassian walnut, well seasoned, is strong but easily fashioned and can be given a very good finish. Specialist manufacturers will supply properly fitting grips if supplied with a plan of the hand with dimensions. These can be supplied in plastic or wood. On the whole, wood is preferred as it will give a better feel to the hand, especially to those who perspire freely. Grips may be chequered to get a better contact with the hand, as it is necessary to have the greatest possible surface of the hand in contact with the grip. A polished surface on the part of the grip which comes into contact with the hand is to be avoided as the hand will slip. A well-made grip is not only functional but adds to the appearance of the gun.

The novice shooter should wait until he has mastered the elements of shooting before he attempts to make himself grips. If he starts too early on this task it will absorb too much of the attention he should be paying to learning the techniques. Overemphasis on his grips may disguise faults in other directions. A good grip is essential for constant high scores but not essential in learning to shoot.

It was stated that the pistol when raised should be naturally aligned on the target. The essence here is to get the correct angle between the rake of the grip and the line of the barrel so that the hand is as far as possible in a natural position. Some pistols are designed so that they are held with the hand angled down at the wrist, others with the hand straight with the wrist. An examination of the gun and the accompanying literature will show which is the correct position. The grip will be made to conform. If when the pistol is brought on aim, an effort has to be made to bring the barrel parallel to the line of sight, then the angle of the grip is wrong. It is not an easy task to get the angle perfect but it is more important to get this right than any fancy finish.

To summarize, the grip should:
(1) fit as much of the surface of the hand as possible;
(2) be made so that the identical hold is taken every time;
(3) be at the correct angle to the gun; and
(4) be held firmly but not tightly with the trigger finger free.

5

Aiming and Firing

Having taken the correct stance and grip, the next stage is to take a proper aim and then release the trigger. The correct aim is the vital part of a good shot. For all practical purposes, the shot will hit the target at the point at which the gun was pointed at the moment it was fired. To make sure that it hits the desired point is another matter and one that requires the co-ordination of eye and muscle to release the trigger when the correct aim is apparent to the eye.

The basic principles of the aim are to position the foresight in the centre of the backsight with the tip of the foresight level with the shoulders of the backsight and then to place this picture on to the target in the correct place. The pistol sights consist of a blade foresight fixed either directly to the top of the front end of the barrel or on a block in that position. When viewed from behind it will appear to the eye as a vertical rectangle, but may have various shapes when viewed from the side. The backsight is either fixed to the rear end of the barrel or to the frame of the pistol behind the end of the barrel. It will consist of a rectangle not more than about 1 inch in width and in the middle of the top there will be a notch through which the foresight is viewed. The notch will either be square or semi-circular. This sight may be firmly fixed to the pistol but is more usually adjustable laterally and vertically by means of spring-locked screws whose adjustment in clicks is defined.

When the pistol is raised to the aiming position, it will almost be a natural aim if the stance and grip are correct. That is, the

AIMING AND FIRING

line of sight will need little adjustment to bring the sights into their proper relationship. The foresight must be positioned in the centre of the backsight with an equal amount of light on either side and the top of the foresight level with the top of the backsight. The sight picture so obtained must then be placed against the target in the proper position. The normal aiming mark is a black disc with a white background. This aiming mark should appear just above the sights leaving a small line of white between the top of the foresight and the aiming mark.* There are circumstances when this is not applicable, particularly when the target is wholly of one colour as in silhouette shooting, but this will be dealt with in the chapter on rapid fire.

It has been widely accepted that the eye should focus on the target and that the sights should be brought into line between the eye and the target. This is wrong; THE EYE MUST FOCUS ON THE TOP OF THE FORESIGHT. As the Plate 17 shows, it is impossible for the eye to focus on three objects at different distances from

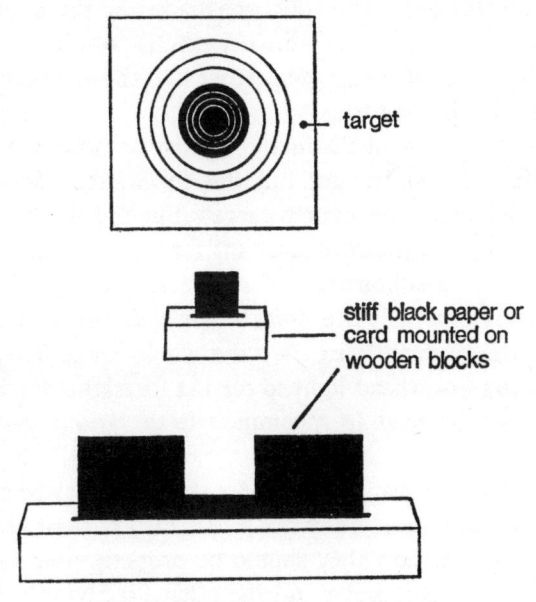

3. *Model for demonstrating aim*

* See note at end of chapter.

the eye at the same time. It is vital that the foresight is sharp and *it does not matter if the target appears blurred*. The eye will distinguish between the black of the aiming mark and the white of the target even though it is not in focus. But the eye cannot position the foresight in the right place if the foresight is blurred.

If the shooter's eyesight is defective any corrective measures should enable the eye to be focussed on the foresight. It is sometimes difficult to explain this to the oculist, but he should understand that the shooter wishes absolute clarity at a precise distance from the eye. Before going to the oculist measure the distance from the eye to the foresight whilst the pistol is in the aim.

It will be found that shooting in different intensities of light has a bearing on the clarity of the foresight. If the light on the target is very bright then there will be too much light from the target coming into the eye and it will be difficult to focus the foresight. This can be rectified by introducing light intensity reducing filters in front of the eye and/or by using an iris with a small aperture. Some apertures are made like the natural iris of the eye in that they can be adjusted exactly to suit the light. It is best to use the largest size of aperture that the eye can accommodate without discomfort.

To see the foresight distinctly it must be illuminated, this is normal for outdoor ranges but not for indoor. Many indoor ranges have brilliantly lighted targets but the firing point is in darkness. In these circumstances the foresight cannot be focused but appears as a silhouette against the target. The shooter will find that his eyes will tire quickly when shooting in such conditions. It is preferable to have the whole range adequately lit with sufficient overhead light to see the foresight clearly, so that the eye does not have to accommodate to various intensities of light.

The eyes are delicate instruments that must not be allowed to undergo undue strain. They can be relieved of some strain if the shooter considers how they should be properly used for aiming. One eye is used for seeing and the other for giving perspective. The eye that sees is the dominant eye and this can be determined by simple experiment. Make a ring with the forefinger and thumb

AIMING AND FIRING

and with this ring about 15 inches in front of the eyes look at a small object which can be seen through the ring with both eyes open. Keeping the ring in the same position, close one eye and then the other. The object will be seen with one eye but not the other. The one that sees the object through the ring is the dominant eye. The shooter will normally use his dominant eye when aiming. He may shoot with his right hand but aim with the left eye. This will make a slight difference to the shape of the grip and the shooter should establish which is his dominant eye before he starts to adjust his grips.

Most people shoot with monocular vision, that is they keep the dominant eye open and close the other eye. The natural tendency will be for the closed eye to open rather than the open eye to close. It will need a conscious effort to keep the one eye closed; this imposes a strain on the closed eye and will disturb the concentration. There are two ways to overcome this strain and both involve keeping both eyes open. One method is to obscure the non-aiming eye by putting a dark or transluscent disc in front of it. The dark disc may be a small black spot on the lense in a line between the pupil and the target. The transluscent disc will allow an equal amount of light to reach each eye. The other ideal method is binocular vision. The dominant eye looks at the sight picture and the other eye is unconsciously inhibited. This method can be achieved quite quickly by practice, especially if the shooter has not already got into the monocular habit. Binocular vision is the most restful form and the vision of the 'seeing' eye is sharpened by the peripheral vision of the 'non-seeing' eye. Even if the shooter is in the habit of using monocular vision, he can try this method by concentration. Many shooters use it anyway when spotting through the telescope.

The light from the sights and target will be received by the eye and the picture falling on the retina will be received by the brain. If the shooting is indoors with no light on the sights, then the eye will receive no light from the sights but only from the light coming over the sights. It will therefore not have as much information as when the whole area is illuminated. The brain has been conditioned and will have a memory of the correct sight picture.

AIMING AND FIRING

It will compare the picture being received with the memory and if the sight picture appears correct, the gun will be fired.

There will be a time lag between the time of recognition and time of firing. The brain having received the picture and compared it with the memory must then initiate the reaction that will pass to the trigger finger to finally release the shot. With training this reaction time can be measured at about a twentieth of a second, i.e. a twentieth of a second will elapse between the time the brain has recognized the sight picture as correct and the finger has pressed the trigger. There will have to be added to this the time taken for the mechanical action of the trigger to fire the cartridge and for the bullet to travel up and leave the barrel. So although the sight picture has been assessed, it will take time for the shot to leave the barrel and the pistol must be held steady during this time. If the pistol wanders off aim there is nothing the shooter can do about it. It is important, therefore, that the aim should be maintained until after the shot has been fired; this will ensure that the aim is steady during that vital time when the shooter has reacted to the correct sight picture. This is known as 'follow through' and it is recognized in any sport that the continuance of any action or stroke is just as important as the initiation of the action or delivery of the stroke.

In the aim the pistol has to be held at arm's length with the elbow straight to give stability to the arm. The weight of the pistol is held by the arm, and the arm is held still by the muscles in the shoulder and back. For deliberate ·22 shooting the arm should not be thrust forward but be naturally straight. It is not possible to shoot consistently with a bent arm. The arm must be straight to keep it steady and to absorb the small amount of recoil from the pistol in a consistent direction. The gun will be brought slowly up to the point of aim. Some shooters bring it up to the aiming mark while others bring the aim above the target and let the gun drop into the proper position. There are no advantages in one way over the other except that the upward lift must not be excessive. It is a waste of effort. As the gun is being brought up the trigger finger will be taking the weight of the trigger progressively so that when the picture is correct the

AIMING AND FIRING

trigger can be quickly released. This involves a complex problem. The shooter has trained himself to hold the pistol as still as possible at arm's length and to make minute adjustments of his muscles to give the correct alignment to the sights. Having achieved this, the shooter has to make the trigger finger move and this involves a number of muscles some of which have to contract whilst others extend. Whilst these muscles are moving the remainder have to keep still. All the muscles are controlled by nervous impulses and one can see that the release of a perfect shot is the result of perfect co-ordination between the mind and a large number of muscles. This requires training to educate the mind and the muscles.

The shooter is now in the position to release the shot. He will raise the question of how long an aim should be held. The basic answer will be the shorter the better as the longer the aim is held the more unsteady it will become. In deliberate shooting the shot should be fired between six and twelve seconds from the time the pistol is in the line of sight. If too short a time is taken the result will be a snatched shot and if more than about twelve seconds then the pistol will be becoming unsteady. The concentration on the aim starts as soon as the pistol is lined up and the whole of the concentration will be funnelled on to the foresight. The mind will be emptied of extraneous thought, thinking only of holding the pistol in the correct place while the progressive trigger pressure is applied. Other aspects of technique are at this moment relegated to the unconscious and even the release of the trigger can be an unconscious act. It will be found that a shot fired like this will always be a good one. This is known as the 'surprise shot'.

The actual release of the trigger requires explanation. The *pad* of the forefinger should be used to squeeze the trigger. The pressure should be applied to the trigger in the direction of the movement of the trigger, that is straight to the rear and not to one side. The bearing surface of the trigger can be increased by fitting a trigger shoe. Pressure should be applied to the trigger as soon as it is lifted from the bench and up to 80 per cent of the trigger weight can be taken before the period of intense concentration commences. The beginner should be careful about taking a too early progressive trigger weight. He should begin by not taking trigger pressure until the pistol is in the aiming area but as he gains experience and learns a precise trigger control he can then take the excess weight at an earlier stage. This trigger pressure must be progressive and only relaxed if the sight picture is not correct at the beginning of the concentration. The pistol will be brought down and the whole procedure started again. The release of the trigger must be gentle and smooth as any ragged release will disturb the stability of the pistol at the vital moment of release and a bad shot will be the result. It should be emphasized here that the trigger must be mechanically perfect so that a smooth and positive let off is obtained every time and at a constant weight. Adjustments of the trigger should only be undertaken by the shooter if he is competent to do so. The movement of the trigger can be controlled by means of a trigger stop. The trigger can be tapped and a small adjustable screw inserted to restrict the backward movement of the trigger after it has released the action. The screw is fitted at the back of the trigger and adjusted against the frame to limit the movement. Some pistols are fitted with trigger stops as standard equipment but if they are not, any competent gunsmith will fit one. The effect of having the trigger stop is to create a very positive let off and to avoid any movement of the gun after the trigger has been released.

It has already been stated that the aim must be maintained for a moment after the trigger has been released. The concentration must be maintained and no relaxation of any muscle allowed until after the shot has gone. This follow-through not only allows the shooter to make sure of a steady shot, but prevents him from thinking about and putting into effect the temptation to bring the gun down until after the shot has been fired. When more than one shot is being fired as in rapid fire the concentration must be continuous until after the string has been fired to make sure that the rhythm is not disturbed before the last shot is fired.

There is a further aspect of firing to be considered and that is the function of the lungs. During the actual firing of the shot the breathing must be restrained. If this were not done the pistol

AIMING AND FIRING

would be moving in an arc as the chest expanded and retracted during the breathing, and it would be impossible for the muscle complex to hold it still on aim. The lungs should be partially deflated during the period of concentration as this condition imposes the least strain on the system. Breathing should be continued normally until the shooter is ready to lift up the pistol. Then take a couple of deep breaths to enrich the oxygen in the blood. Then as the shooter is about to begin the concentration period the air should be gently exhaled until the shooter feels comfortable. The lungs must not be fully emptied as this would impose just as much strain as if they were full of air. If the lungs were fully inflated during the firing of the shot, the air would be trying to force its way out and the shooter could not concentrate. Experiment for a moment now: take a deep breath and hold it for fifteen seconds; 1—2—3, etc., 13—14—15. This has required a conscious effort but there is very little effort required with the lungs partially exhaled. Restraining the breathing also has an effect on the time factor for firing the shot. If the shooter tries to hold on too long the system will become slightly starved of oxygen and the pulse rate will increase causing the aim to become unsteady. When the shot has been fired, allow the lungs to fill with air and then take a couple of deep breaths to tone up the system.

This chapter can be summarized as follows:

(1) The foresight in the middle of, and the top of the foresight level with, the shoulders of the backsight;

(2) The eye focusing on the foresight and the sight picture put on to the target slightly under the aiming mark;

(3) Concentrate on the foresight, restrain the breathing and at the same time progressively take the weight of the trigger;

(4) Continue to squeeze the trigger as the correct aim is maintained and as the shot is fired;

(5) Maintain the aim for a moment (follow through).

Note to page 51. A technique known as 'area aiming' which is favoured by experienced shooters is to position the sight picture well down the target, as low as the four ring or below. This will allow greater concentration on the sight relationship and there should be no difficulty in maintaining the distance between the sight picture and the aiming mark. The group should be narrow and slightly elongated but well within the grouping capacity of the shooter.

6

Applying the Principles

Having learned the principles involved in firing the pistol the next stage is active participation and to begin with the novice should concentrate on ·22 calibre deliberate shooting before progressing to other forms of target shooting. It is, of course, essential that the novice starts his shooting under a qualified instructor or an experienced shooter. The instructor must first see that the novice fully understands all the safety precautions and carries them out. It saves a lot of trouble later if good habits are insisted upon from the beginning. Each stage of the techniques should be supervised, the loading of the pistol, taking up and testing the stance, seeing that the right amount of tension is put on the grip and that the trigger is correctly squeezed.

The correct techniques must be assimilated before the instructor allows the novice to fire a shot. This dry training can be made interesting and methods have been devised to simulate actual firing. A dummy pistol can be built with sights and a trigger mechanism so that the novice can be taught in classroom conditions away from the range. A good substitute for a real trigger can be made by adapting the trigger switch from an electric hand tool. The correct aim can be checked by using a small prism or oblique glass placed on top the gun in the line of sight between backsight and foresight. The instructor can, by looking into the oblique glass, check the aim of the pupil and have him make the necessary adjustment to bring the sights into their proper relationships. The proper sight picture will have been demonstrated to the pupil by diagram and model.

APPLYING THE PRINCIPLES

The instructor can guide the pupil in learning the progressive trigger pressure by first placing his finger on the trigger and getting the pupil to put his finger on top if the trigger guard is big enough. The operation can be reversed with the instructor's finger on top of the pupil's and the instructor taking the weight of the trigger.

At about this stage the novice should have the mechanism of the pistol explained to him. The cartridge will be either rim fire or centre fire depending whether the shooter is using ·22 calibre or full bore. The cartridge consists of a metal, usually brass or steel, case containing at the base a primer of which, in centre-fire ammunition, the bottom of a soft copper cup is exposed. With rim fire the priming powder is contained in the rim of the base of the cartridge case. The priming material is sensitive to a sharp blow. The lead bullet is crimped in the case and between the base of the bullet and the primer is the explosive powder which when ignited burns furiously and produces gas under pressure which forces the bullet through the barrel.

The cartridge is inserted into the breech or receiver chamber of a single-shot pistol so that the bullet touches the beginning of the rifling and the base of the cartridge fits accurately against the face of the breech. In some pistols a little pressure is required to force the cartridge home. In this case the bullet is forced gently into the rifling so that when fired it starts from its correct position. The barrel is rifled with two or more spirals or grooves and the flat areas between the grooves are known as lands. The spiral grooves impart a twist to the bullet so that it maintains an accurate course between the barrel and the target. A close examination of this path will reveal that the bullet yaws slightly in flight giving rise to the small group formed even when the gun is fired from a bench rest. The burning of the explosive in the cartridge is designed to give a big initial thrust to the base of the bullet and then an even pressure on its passage down the barrel. As well as imparting pressure to the base of the cartridge there is an equal pressure in the opposite direction against the base of the cartridge case. This gives rise to recoil and is the reason why the pistol must be held firmly during the firing of the shot. In the single-

APPLYING THE PRINCIPLES

shot pistol all the recoil is taken along the straight arm of the shooter but in the self-loading pistol part of this thrust is used to operate the mechanism.

The mode of operation of the auto-loading pistol of the simple 'blow back' type is as follows. The cartridges are fed one by one into the magazine, the platform being pulled down slightly to allow space for each round. The magazine spring will push the cartridges to the top of the magazine into the correct position for the slide or block in its forward movement to feed the cartridge into the breech. The cartridge is then 'locked' home, in different ways depending on the design of the pistol. After the bullet is fired the backward movement of the slide withdraws the empty case with the extractor and in the same stroke throws it clear of the pistol with the ejector. The backward movement of the slide will continue, re-cocking the hammer mechanism and then immediately going forward under the action of the return spring, reloading the breech with the next cartridge from the top of the magazine. The slide is so constructed that the force required to overcome its inertia is not accumulated until the bullet has left the barrel. The actual working of the mechanism appears almost instantaneous to the eye, but it does have a designed time (of approximately one-tenth of a second per cycle). It will be apparent how important it is to see that the working parts are kept clean for the mechanism to function efficiently.

The operation of the trigger mechanism also needs explanation. The primer is ignited by a sharp blow from the end of the firing pin. The end of the firing pin is designed to impart to the base of the cartridge the correct amount of force to ignite the primer. Interference in the shape of or damage to the nose of the firing pin can cause malfunctioning, and if the nose is too small it can even pierce the cartridge. In the automatic the firing pin is usually held back from the base of the cartridge by a small spring. When the pistol is cocked the hammer is held back against a compressed spring by the top end of the trigger engaging in a notch on the base of the hammer. With the single-shot pistol and the revolver, the cocking piece or hammer is similarly held back. The top end of the trigger is known as the 'sear' and the notch on the hammer

APPLYING THE PRINCIPLES

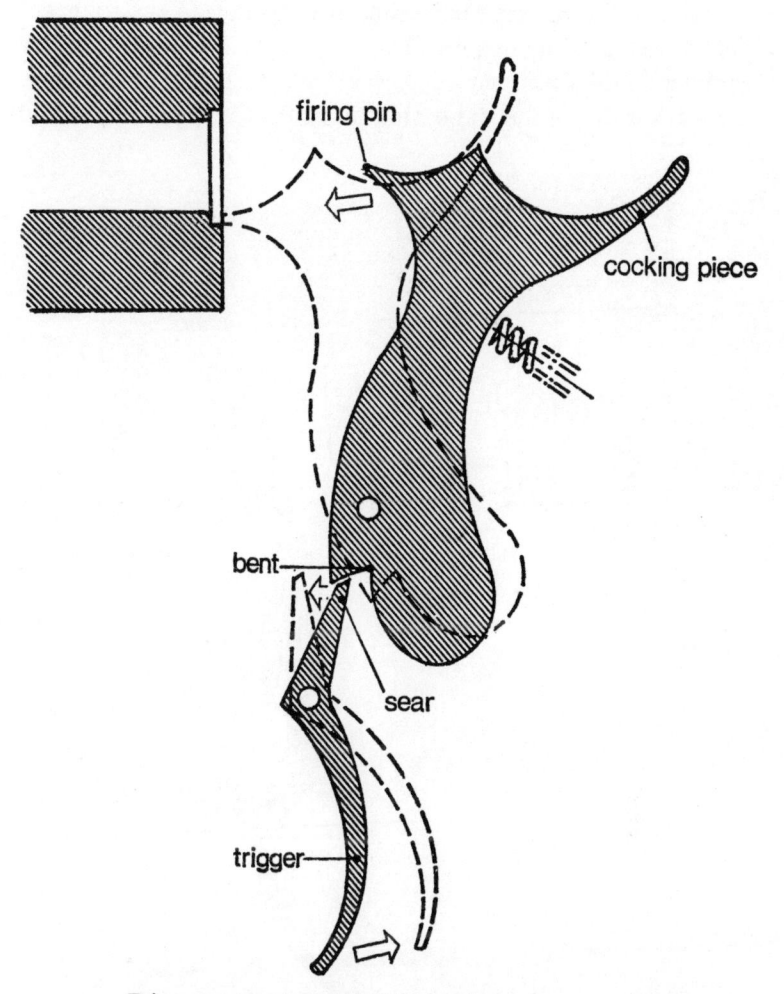

4. Diagrammatic mechanism of single shot pistol

is called the 'bent'. The friction between these two metal surfaces controls the weight required to release the trigger and it is a skilled task to ensure that the two surfaces make good and complete contact without any rough points of contact.

The trigger itself is held forward by a small spring and the strength of this spring will also have some effect on the weight of

APPLYING THE PRINCIPLES

the trigger. To release the hammer the bottom of the trigger is pulled back and the two metal surfaces slide apart, releasing the hammer. This flies forward driven by the energy in the compressed spring. In the single-shot pistol the firing pin on the end

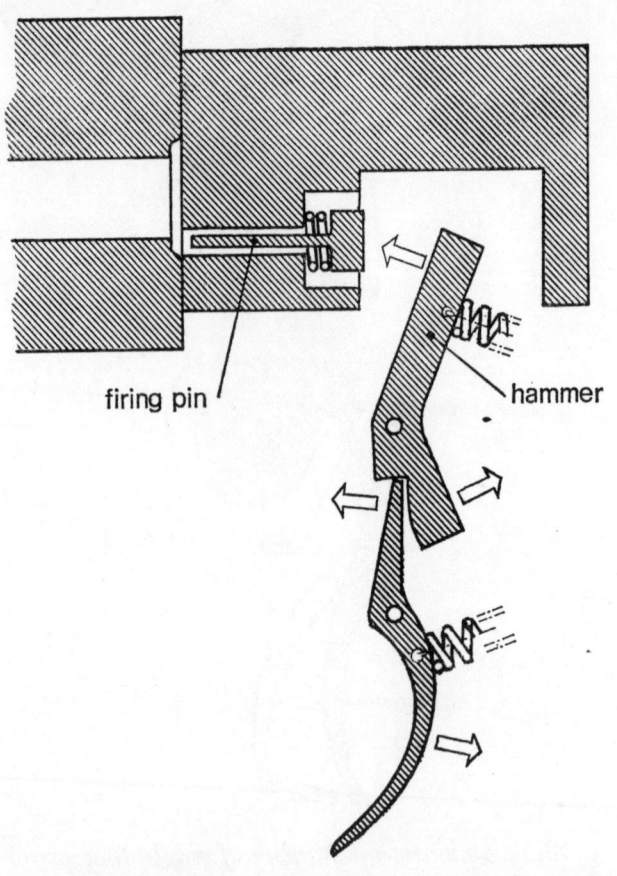

5. Diagrammatic mechanism of automatic pistol

of the hammer strikes the base of the cartridge but in the automatic the hammer strikes the base of the firing pin, thrusting it forward, overriding its weak retracting spring, to ignite the primer.

The normal trigger weight for standard ·22 competitions is

APPLYING THE PRINCIPLES

2 pounds but for centre fire it is 3 pounds and for ladies' standard hand gun it is 1 kilogram. The action of the Free Pistol is similar except that actuating springs and a trip lever are introduced between the trigger and the sear. These can be adjusted so that a load of as little as 5 grams (approximately $\frac{1}{6}$ ounce) will release the trigger.

Several things now become apparent. The mechanism must be kept clean and not over-oiled. Too much oil will cause slip and will attract dirt. The weight required to release the trigger depends very much on the surface area engaged by the sear in the bent. The smoothness of release depends on the relationship between these two surfaces, which should be highly polished. Uneven surfaces and wear will cause drag and the moment of release will be erratic and uncertain. It will also be appreciated that there is a definite time lag between the release of the trigger and the departure of the bullet from the barrel.

The detailed mechanism of the particular make of weapon used by the shooter will be given in the brochure issued by the manufacturer. The novice should be warned that he should be careful in dismantling his pistol and should seek knowledgeable advice before so doing. Although pistols are very robust they are precision built and parts can be easily damaged through carelessness and ignorance.

The novice should now be ready to fire his first shot and if he has learned the principles and basic techniques then he should be confident that he will make a success of his first effort. The instructor must keep firm control at this stage; he should make sure that the novice has taken up the correct position and that the range is clear; he will then give the order 'Load'.

The key to success in all shooting is the ability to group successive shots in a circle of as small diameter as possible. It must be assumed that the gun and ammunition are capable of grouping and continue to remain so. With this assumption success only depends on the shooter grouping to the best of his ability and the smaller his group the higher will be his scores. At no stage in the shooter's career will he be able to equal the grouping capacity of his gun or ammunition.

APPLYING THE PRINCIPLES

When the novice starts his group will be very large and he should therefore start shooting at a short range. This should not be more than 20 yards and if it is found that he cannot fire a group of target size at this distance, the target should be brought forward until he can see all his shots hitting the target. The distance can then be quickly increased to 20 yards. It is better to learn to shoot at 20 yards rather than at a shorter distance, at which it is more difficult to detect errors on the target owing to the spread of shot. It may take a number of visits to the range before the novice gets ten consecutive shots on the target at 20 yards. This is not important at this stage if it can be impressed on him that progress in this sport can be slow. Slow progress with a sure foundation is a better course than rapid progress with uncertain foundation. On his first visit it will suffice if only ten shots are fired and it does not matter if there is no target. The shooter has to get the feel of the gun firing a live cartridge before he need think about where the shot should be going. He should point the gun in a safe direction down the range.

For some time the instructor should see that the amount of shooting done by the novice is restricted, and it should not exceed thirty rounds in a session. The muscles are not attuned to the strain and have to be educated. Far more harm will be done if too much rather than too little shooting is tried too early. But the limited amount of shooting should be earnestly performed so that from the start the shooter is impressed with the fact that when he starts competition shooting the same effort must go into each shot over the whole of the shoot. Each shot is a match of its own with the maximum score for each shot as the desirable goal.

The trainee should start his shooting by trying to achieve a group, and some pattern will emerge fairly early. It does not matter where the centre of the group is situated so long as it is somewhere on the target. The young shot is always anxious to shoot for a score and to score tens. This is a worthy objective but it should be pointed out to him that tens will come far quicker if he learns to group first and to forget the bull's-eyes in the early stages.

It is quite likely to begin with that the new shot is using a

15. Author on aim. Shooting right-handed but using left eye so that pistol has to be brought further across the body. Note: peaked cap, ear muffs, shooting glasses and finger off trigger.

16. Author's son. Right-handed using right eye. Compare position with plate 15.

17. The Aim, as seen by the eye. Backsight clear but not sharp. Foresight very sharp, target out of focus.

18. Hämmerli CO2 Pistol (·177 calibre) (*S. A. Hämmerli*)

APPLYING THE PRINCIPLES

borrowed or club gun with factory grips and few of the refinements associated with the weapons of the expert. This is unimportant at this stage as the shooter is learning the basic techniques and refinements can come when he really starts to shoot on his own. He will then experiment in all sorts of ways.

After about a couple of months the group should be down to about 6 inches. The group should now be moved so that its centre coincides with the centre of the target. It is, of course, essential that the novice should use the same gun the whole time. When the group is in the centre the shooter can then start shooting for a score but at the same time he must remember he is always shooting a group.

To move the centre of the group the sights must be moved. It is impossible to lay down hard and fast rules as to how much sights are moved as this varies from weapon to weapon depending on the sight radius of the pistol. The simpler types of sights have to be driven with a punch whilst the more sophisticated ones move in $\frac{1}{4}$ minute clicks. Some pistols have fixed backsights and foresights and very little lateral alteration can be made. Such pistols should not be used for serious target shooting. More modern pistols do have sights that are capable of movement, laterally by means of the backsight and vertically either by adjusting the foresight or backsight.

Backsights if they do not have laterally adjusting screws are mitred and can be driven sideways with a punch. This is rather a hit or miss arrangement and the final adjustment is by trial and error. Screw adjustments can be defined either by learning how much a half or whole turn of the screw will move the group or how much each click will move the group. This should be noted.

Vertical adjustment can also be made on the backsight. This is done either by the block on which the backsight is mounted being raised or lowered on a screw thread or if the backsight is on a spring leaf an adjusting screw can alter its tension. If, however, the backsight is fixed then vertical adjustments have to be made with the foresight. Some foresights can be pivoted so that the rearward tip of the foresight can be raised or lowered. Pistols with fixed foresights and fixed backsights can only be adjusted

APPLYING THE PRINCIPLES

vertically by filing the sights and once metal is removed it is difficult to replace.

The alteration of sights does need explanation to the novice.

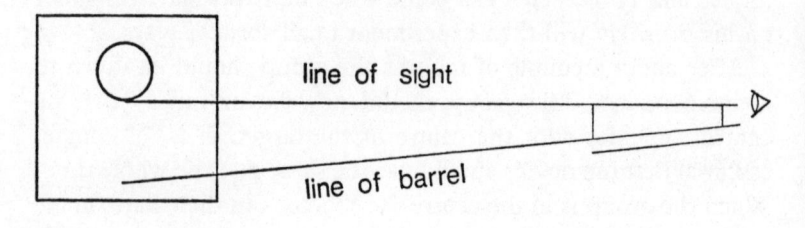

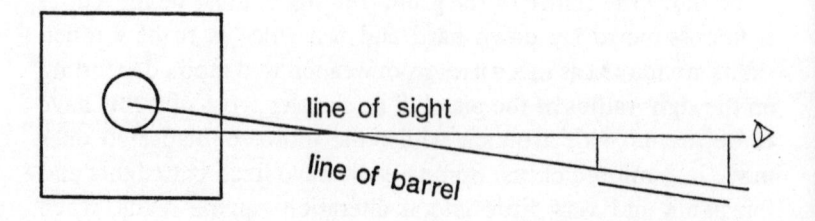

Same foresight : higher backsight

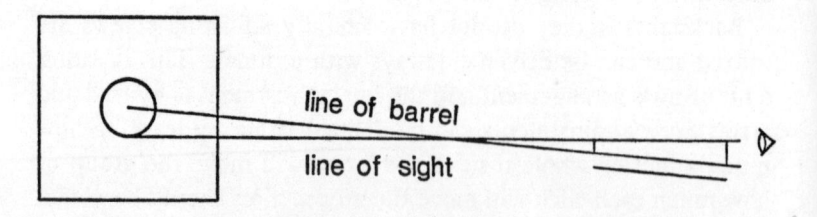

Shorter foresight : same backsight

6. Correction of elevation

The line of sight passes from the eye, through the notch in the backsight, over the foresight to the target. If this line is coincidental with the line of fire through the barrel then the shots will virtually strike the target where they are aimed. The line of

APPLYING THE PRINCIPLES

sight will remain constant and therefore the line of fire, i.e. the line of the barrel, has to be altered. If the shots are low the angle of the barrel line has to be lifted. This is done either by raising

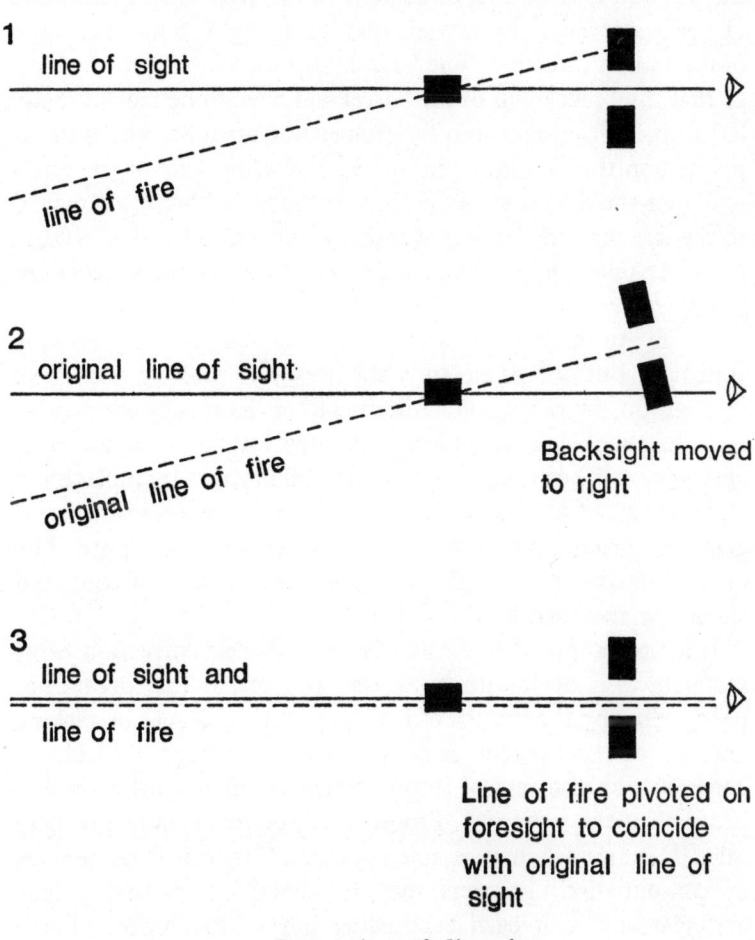

1
line of sight
line of fire

2
original line of sight
original line of fire

Backsight moved to right

3
line of sight and
line of fire

Line of fire pivoted on foresight to coincide with original line of sight

7. Correction of direction

the backsight and therefore lowering the breech end of the gun or by lowering the foresight and raising the fore-end of the barrel. Both achieve the same object as is shown by the diagram. The opposite will apply if the group is high.

APPLYING THE PRINCIPLES

A similar method is used for determining the way sights have to be moved to alter the lateral adjustment of the group. The eye is in a fixed place looking through the sights. If the group is to the left and it is desired to move it to the right then the muzzle of the barrel has to be moved from left to right to move the line of fire in that direction. The backsight is then moved to the right so that the breech end of the barrel will have to be moved to the left to bring the sight into the proper line of sight. The pistol is pivoted on the foresight and movements at the rear of the pistol will alter the direction of the shot. If the group has to be moved to the left then the backsight must be moved to the left. *Always move the sights in the direction in which it is desired to move the group.*

Sights are made to be used. This may sound a very obvious statement but one often finds shooters who will try and move their groups by aiming off. 'Aiming off' or 'Kentucky windage' is very unreliable and should only be used for the odd shot in an emergency. When the group does not fall in the correct place and all other causes have been checked, e.g. faulty stance, inconsistent grip, the group should be moved by moving the sights. The normal setting of the sights is known as the 'zero' setting and should be recorded by the shooter.

It is not proposed to discuss faults and their correction here; this subject is dealt with in another chapter. If the shooter has been following the lessons of his instructor he should be making gradual but consistent improvement. It is very difficult to generalize on the rate of improvement as no two shooters will progress at the same rate. Progress will be made although there may be times when it is not apparent. These will be periods of consolidation. Progress may be described as having hills and plateaux with each succeeding hill a little higher. There may be the odd valley but the next hill will always be a little higher.

Having learned to group the shooter will apply himself to shoot for a score. He should keep a record of each shoot so that he can chart his progress. He should start to shoot in competition at his own level. There will be club competitions, graded and

APPLYING THE PRINCIPLES

handicap events and he will always be shooting against his own best score. After a short time he will have an average score to shoot for and improve upon.

Except for the first practice card, all cards should be fired as competition cards. The practice card enables him to adjust himself to the conditions, see that the gun is shooting at its proper zero, and if not to make adjustments. After that, each card is a match, if only against some standard that the shooter or his instructor has set. This standard must always be within the capability of the shooter. His shooting will fluctuate either side of his average but will be fairly close to it. Assuming that he is shooting within the 6 ring, his score would be about 72. As an example, he fires his card and his first five shots all score tens. His last five shots would, according to his average, only score about 25, i.e. 4, 6, 7, 8 and one off the target. This would not be a case for shedding tears as the score is above his average. As his average increases and he begins to get more shots in the middle the shots will fluctuate in this manner. Many shooters seem despondent when this happens, but it would be even more extraordinary if the shooter were to fire another five tens!

If at any time the shooting appears to have really become static then the shooter should go back to basic principles and make a critical examination (if possible with his instructor) of each of his actions to see that he is carrying out the correct procedure. There is, of course, always room for experiment, but this should never be made in the middle of a match or before an important competition. Experiment should be attempted when there is time to do so and time to regain the previous conditions if the experiment fails. Notes should be kept of the experiment attempted and of the results obtained. The kind of experiment depends on the attitude of the shooter towards the sport. Some shooters are concerned with specializing on a particular course of fire and will try different stances and grips but using the same gun. Others will see how many different weapons they can use. Any serious intention will give the shooter maximum interest and pleasure even though he will not necessarily produce high scores. Other shooters will attempt to achieve high scores and will ex-

APPLYING THE PRINCIPLES

periment with guns to find the one that suits them best for their particular purpose.

When the shooter has settled down to shooting scores of between 75 and 80 he will start to consider each shot as a match on its own. (The score mentioned applies to N.S.R.A. standard targets at 20 yards.) Each shot will be planned carefully taking into account any errors detected in the previous shot. He should go through each action deliberately—check his stance, grip the pistol in the same way for each shot—go through in his mind the correct relationship of the sights when on aim and then when he has composed himself bring the pistol up on aim. As he concentrates on the foresight he is progressively squeezing the trigger and when the aim is within his margin of error the pressure will be continued and the shot fired. The shooter should by this time know where the pistol is pointing at the time the shot is fired. Before looking at the target through the telescope he should declare his aim as the pistol was fired. The shooter should have a diagram on which he records his call before spotting the shot. When he then spots the shot he should note the position on the same diagram. If the shot did not go near his declared point of aim then he must analyse the error and find a reason for it. His instructor or coach will be able to help him at this stage by watching his actions when shooting. If the declared shot is well away from the centre the aim must have been very bad and the shot should not have been fired. There is no excuse for any shot outside the normal group of the shooter, except carelessness. The shooter should be in sufficient control of his techniques to see that the shot is going to be a bad one and to relax and remove the trigger finger and bring the pistol down to the bench. He must do this each time until he is satisfied that the shot will be within his group.

By keeping a record of the strike of the shots on the target the firer will find that his errors will tend to form themselves in groups. The method of rectifying faults is described in a later chapter. It can be shown that certain errors are caused by faulty techniques and with care can be corrected. Time will improve the shooting of the novice and he will reach the stage when he

APPLYING THE PRINCIPLES

will want to examine more sophisticated techniques which will bring his shooting into the top standards. Advanced shooting will be dealt with separately.

The routine of the shooter at this stage can be summarized by the phrases which are prominently displayed at the Advanced Marksmanship Unit of the United States Army:

> PREPARE FOR SHOT
> PLAN SHOT
> RELAX BEFORE SHOT
> DELIVER SHOT
> ANALYSE ERROR
> CORRECT ERROR

If every shooter had this stuck into his shooting box for a constant reminder there would be far fewer loose shots and scores would improve rapidly.

Scores will also improve if the shooter has a methodical training programme. The weekly visit to the range is not by itself sufficient to maintain or improve a standard. If the shooter is keen he will take every opportunity of practice without firing live ammunition. This is called 'dry practice'. It can be done at home or in any convenient place but it should be taken seriously and as much care put into it as into a match. It is preferable to 'fire' ten shots very carefully than thirty without attention. There is no need to put up a target, just choose a spot on the wall at the right height and practise aiming and firing. If actually cocking the weapon care should be taken to insert an empty cartridge case in the chamber to prevent damage to the firing pin. It is essential that every safety precaution should be taken even when dry firing. Various aspects of firing can be separately practised—one day make sure that the stance is correct, another day see that the aim is being correctly taken and another day practise the trigger let off.

Live practice can be simulated by using an air pistol. The modern continental air pistol is a very accurate weapon and even at 20 yards compares very favourably with the ·22 weapon, though the competition distance is 10 metres. It is very valuable as a training aid as it gives a positive answer to the shooter's action. They can be fired indoors with safety if proper precautions are taken and a bullet catcher is provided. If fitted with proper match sights they can almost exactly duplicate the weapon which is being practised. They can also be adapted to simulate rapid-fire shooting. It must always be remembered that an air pistol is not a toy and a pellet can inflict a very nasty injury. Practice with an air pistol or dry firing should be as frequent as possible, but not overdone. About thirty careful shots each session are sufficient to practise the techniques and keep muscles and reactions toned up.

Air Pistol shooting is very popular in Europe and from 1st January 1968 has been included in the U.I.T. list of matches. The match is shot at 10 metres, the ten ring is 12 millimetres, increasing in width by 8 millimetres for each ring, giving a total diameter of 156 millimetres. The Air Pistol may be any air or CO_2 pistol with a calibre of 4·5 millimetres (·177 inches). The pistol must not weigh more than 1,500 grams; it must not exceed 200 millimetres in height, 420 millimetres in length and 50 millimetres in width. The trigger pressure must not be less than 500 grams and set triggers are not allowed. The match is of 40 shots and 10 sighting shots are permitted. Ninety minutes are allowed to fire the match, including sighters. It is expected that this competition will prove very popular.

7

Fault Analysis and Correction

This is a difficult subject to consider because errors can be caused by so many factors acting in combination or by themselves. If the firer never made any errors, then all his shots would fall within the grouping capacity of his gun and ammunition, and his own capacity to hold the gun. This would lead to an intolerable position as all shooters would be making very high scores and there would no longer be any incentive. Pistol shooting is fascinating because the targets used make very high scores uncommon.

It is a basic fact that the bullet will strike the target at the point at which the pistol was aiming at the moment the bullet left the barrel. But to every rule there are exceptions and two can be considered in this case. The first exception is faulty ammunition. This is unusual but it can happen and it is either a fault in the bullet itself or in the load. A bad bullet will yaw wildly in flight and its point of impact will be anywhere. For the good shot this will certainly be apparent as the shot will be far from the declared point of aim. One cannot foresee such an occurrence unless the shooter is using hand-loaded ammunition, when the remedy is in his own hands. The second exception will be a fault in the weapon and this may or may not be the responsibility of the firer. Even the most experienced shot has been known to miss the obvious when his group is not forming or is wrongly positioned. The first step is to check the weapon; examine it externally to see if there has been some accidental shift in the sights or if they have come loose. This check should always be made before starting a

FAULT ANALYSIS AND CORRECTION

shoot, but it can be overlooked. Sights have even been known to fall off during a shoot!

The more usual fault in the gun is that lead is wiped from the bullet during its passage down the barrel and lodges on the

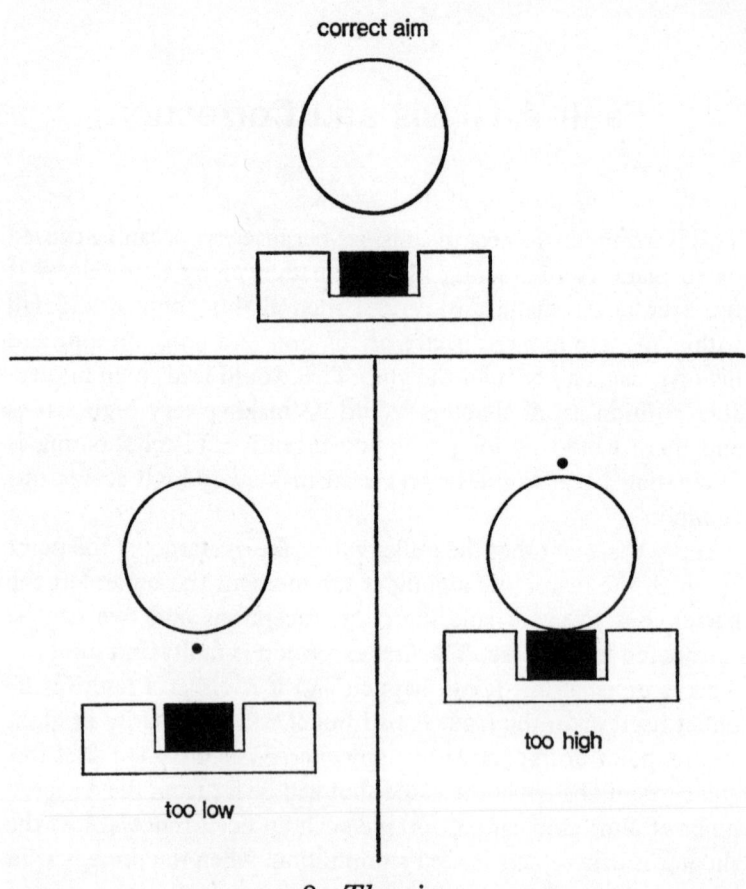

correct aim

too low

too high

8. *The aim*

surface of the lands and in the grooves. The following shots scatter. This can happen in the middle of a shoot even though the barrel was cleaned immediately before the shooting started. It is prone to happen in conditions of high temperature and humidity.

If, therefore, a shot is fired which does not strike the target

FAULT ANALYSIS AND CORRECTION

close to the declared aim and there is no fault in the firer's technique, and the gun appears in order externally, the barrel should be cleaned. This may happen in the middle of an important match but it does not take long to clean and inspect the barrel. Many experienced shooters clean their pistols during a shoot even though there is no apparent lack of accuracy.

The vast majority of shots which do not hit the target close to the centre are not the fault of either the gun or the ammunition; they occur because the firer himself has made an error. This should be apparent at the time to the shooter who should analyse the cause of the error and take steps to see that it does not happen again. Although not a fault of technique, the biggest cause of shooting errors is lack of concentration. This will be discussed in a later chapter.

To consider faults in technique it is necessary to divide shooters into two categories, those who are still learning the techniques and those who have established their methods. Whilst there are basic principles which apply to all shooters, they will all develop their own minor variations which they have found suit themselves best. It is unusual to find an established shot who changes his techniques unless he is forced to do so by some physical disability.

There are certain patterns of group which will indicate to the coach or instructor that the firer is committing certain faults. This is best illustrated by diagrams.

In diagram 9 the group is elongated vertically. The diagrams are exaggerated to illustrate the fault. The vertically elongated group is due either to the incorrect position of the foresight in relation to the backsight or incorrect positioning of the sight picture in the vertical direction. If the foresight is above the level of the backsight the shot will go high and if the foresight is below the level of the backsight, then the shot will be low.

If the foresight is correctly positioned within the backsight but there is too much white of the target showing between the sights and the aiming mark, the shot will again be low. Conversely if the sights move too close to the aiming mark or into the black itself, then the shot will go high. If the sights do appear against the

FAULT ANALYSIS AND CORRECTION

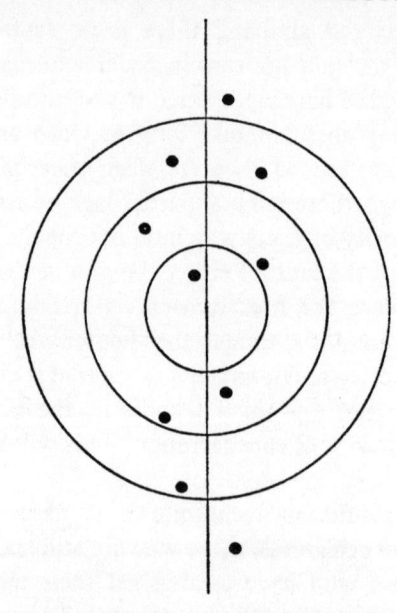

9. *Vertically elongated group*

Group formed with varying heights of foresight or inconsistent amount of white between sights and aiming mark.

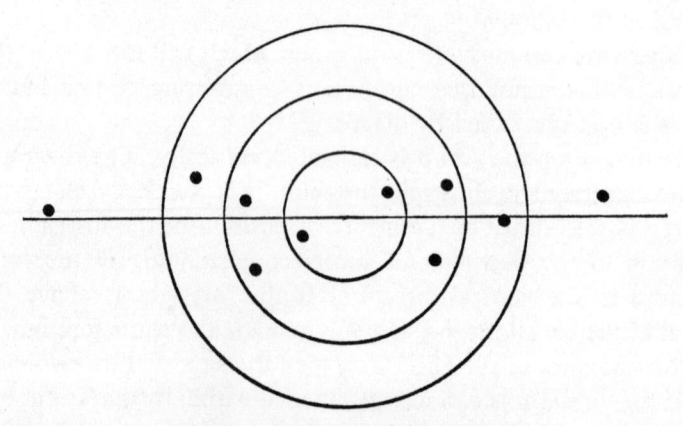

10. *Laterally elongated group*

Group formed when foresight is incorrectly centred in backsight or the sight pisture is incorrectly centred.

FAULT ANALYSIS AND CORRECTION

black of the aiming mark it will be more difficult to determine the vertical deflection of the bullet.

In diagram 10 the group is elongated laterally; this is because either the foresight has been incorrectly centred in the backsight or the shooter is not taking the sight picture on the vertical centre line of the target. If the foresight is too much to the left,

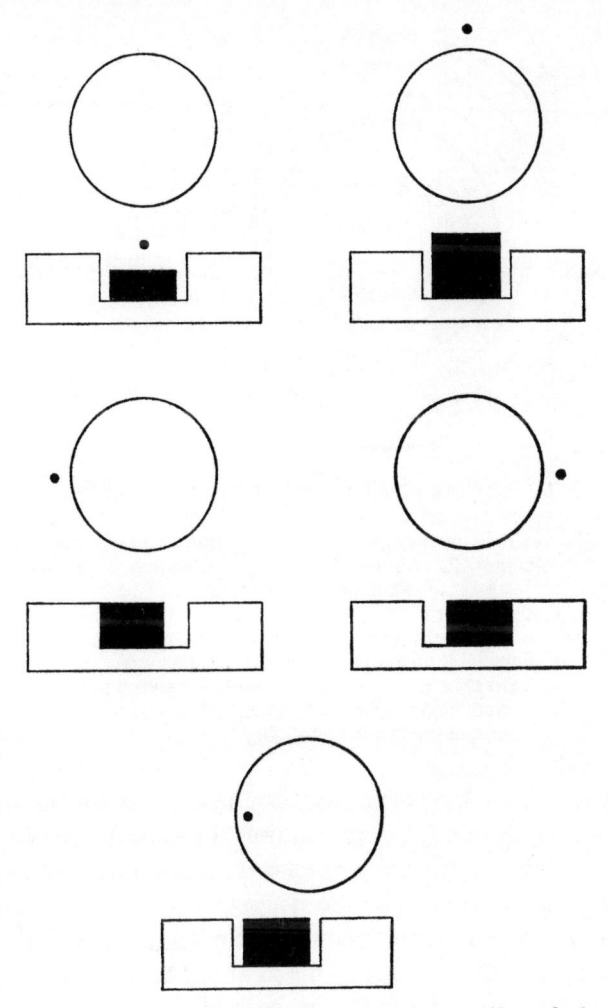

11. *Incorrect sight pictures showing strike of shot*

FAULT ANALYSIS AND CORRECTION

then the shot will go to the left and vice versa. The amount of light on each side of the foresight must be equal. This may sometimes be difficult, especially on outdoor ranges, when there is more illumination on one side of the foresight than on the other. The group will be displaced towards the side that the brighter light is coming from.

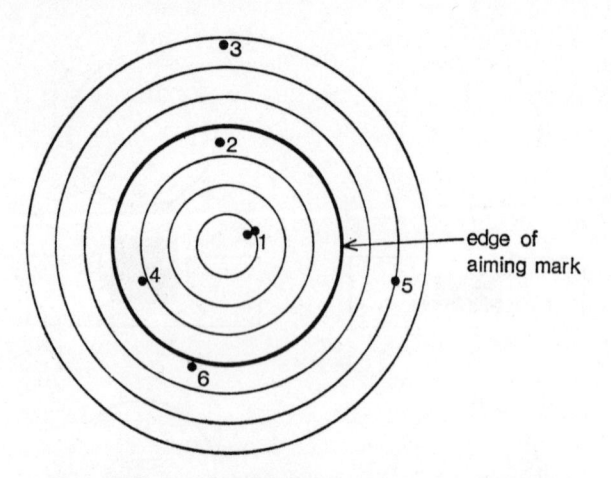

12. *Effect of deliberate errors in sighting*

Target fired by author making deliberate sighting errors. Single shot .22 Webley, 2 lb trigger. Distance 20 yards. Standard NSRA target
1. Correct aim
2. Correct sight relationship too close to aiming mark
3. Foresight too high and touching aiming mark
4. Correct height – foresight incorrectly centred to left
5. Correct height – foresight incorrectly centred to right
6. Foresight too low in backsight.

Faults in the taking of the aim can be corrected if the shooter goes over in his mind, before he raises the gun, the correct sight picture and does not fire the pistol if the aim is incorrect. Aiming is made easier if the grip has been adjusted so that when the firer raises the gun he is almost taking a natural aim. He will then not have to use any effort to line up the sights. 'The foresight correctly positioned in the middle of the backsight and the top of the foresight level with the shoulders of the backsight'. This must be

FAULT ANALYSIS AND CORRECTION

repeated mentally by the shooter for every shot. This correct relationship is then placed on the target so that there is a little strip of white between the top of the foresight and the aiming

1 Correct sight relationship

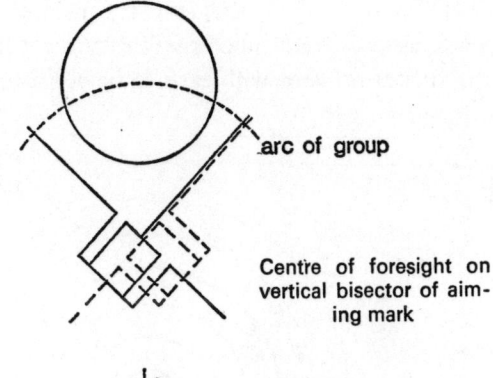

arc of group

Centre of foresight on vertical bisector of aiming mark

2 Incorrect sight relationship

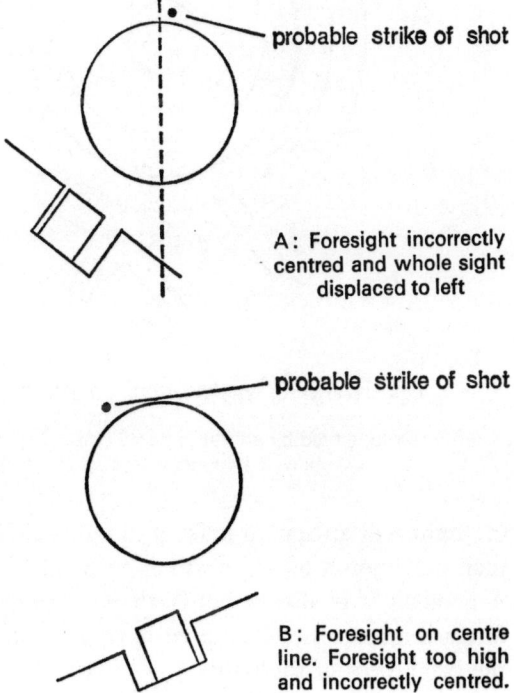

probable strike of shot

A: Foresight incorrectly centred and whole sight displaced to left

probable strike of shot

B: Foresight on centre line. Foresight too high and incorrectly centred.

13. *The effect of cant*

FAULT ANALYSIS AND CORRECTION

mark. If this strip is too narrow then there is the danger that the aim will slip up into the black and a high shot will result. If too much white is taken it is difficult to judge consistently and the group will be vertically shaped. A reasonable distance below the aiming mark is about the next scoring ring. The actual amount of white used by each shooter will vary according to the shooter, but the successful shot will learn to be consistent. The brightness of

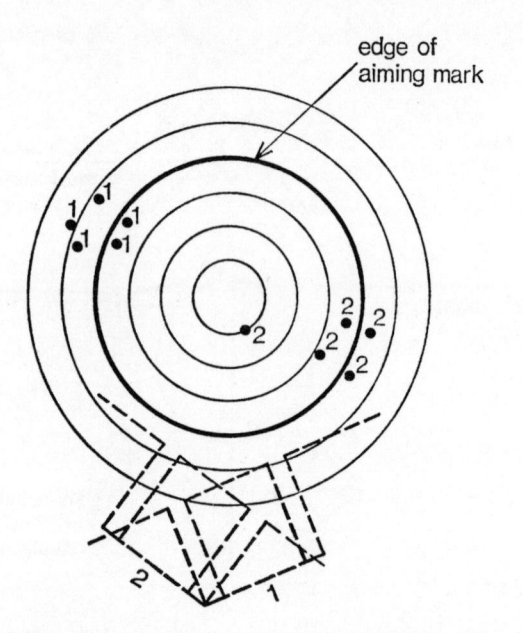

14. *Result of experiment to show effect of cant*

Groups fired by author to show effect of Cant. Single shot Webley. 2 lb trigger weight. Distance 20 yards

the light will appear to make a difference. If the light is glaring then the amount of white will appear to be bigger than required. A good light is always better than a bright light, but coloured filters can help the shooter to have a constant picture whatever the brightness of the light.

The correct sight picture will follow, remembering the most important rule about aiming and that the eye must be focused

FAULT ANALYSIS AND CORRECTION

on the foresight and not allowed to wander from the sights to the target.

Another aiming factor that will alter the position of the strike of the bullet is CANT. This is leaning the pistol away from the vertical. If, however, the correct sight relation is maintained the cant has to be pronounced before the displacement of the shot is considerable. The strike of the shot will be in the direction of the line through the centre of the barrel and the centre of the foresight. If there is any tendency to cant it will be towards the left. If the foresight has been extended then the effect of cant will be greater. If the sights relationship is incorrect then the error on the target will be much greater, as shown in the diagram. Many shots in international class cant but they are very consistent in their hold and any displacement due to this feature has been compensated by sight adjustment or remedied by adjustment to grip.

There are some interesting facts that are relevant to aiming and which will help the shooter to understand the importance of the correct relationship of the sights. The size of the group depends on the ability of the shooter to maintain a consistent hold and to fire his shots within his known error of aim. *It is impossible to hold the pistol absolutely still.* The mere fact of the blood pulsing through the arm will induce a slight tremor in the hand and the foresight will move through a small arc. After the shooter has achieved some skill, he will recognize his own arc of movement and will know that if he fires within this arc he will get the result he expects. Changes in this arc of movement can be very simply demonstrated. Take a couple of minutes vigorous exercise and then try and hold the pistol still. Even when pulse and breathing rate have returned to normal it is doubtful if the minimum arc of movement can be held and it will take some time until it is reduced to the shooter's minimum. The effect on the target of the arc of movement can be demonstrated either by bringing the target to the end of the barrel or by making the barrel as long as the range (in imagination, of course!). The movement described will pivot from the shoulder and any movement in the foresight will only be increased in proportion to the distance from the

A — Correct

A — Correct relationship between sights. Low aim — Low Shot

Parallel error

X — Incorrect relationship between sights. Foresight below level of backsight. Low shot although backsight is at correct height

Angular error

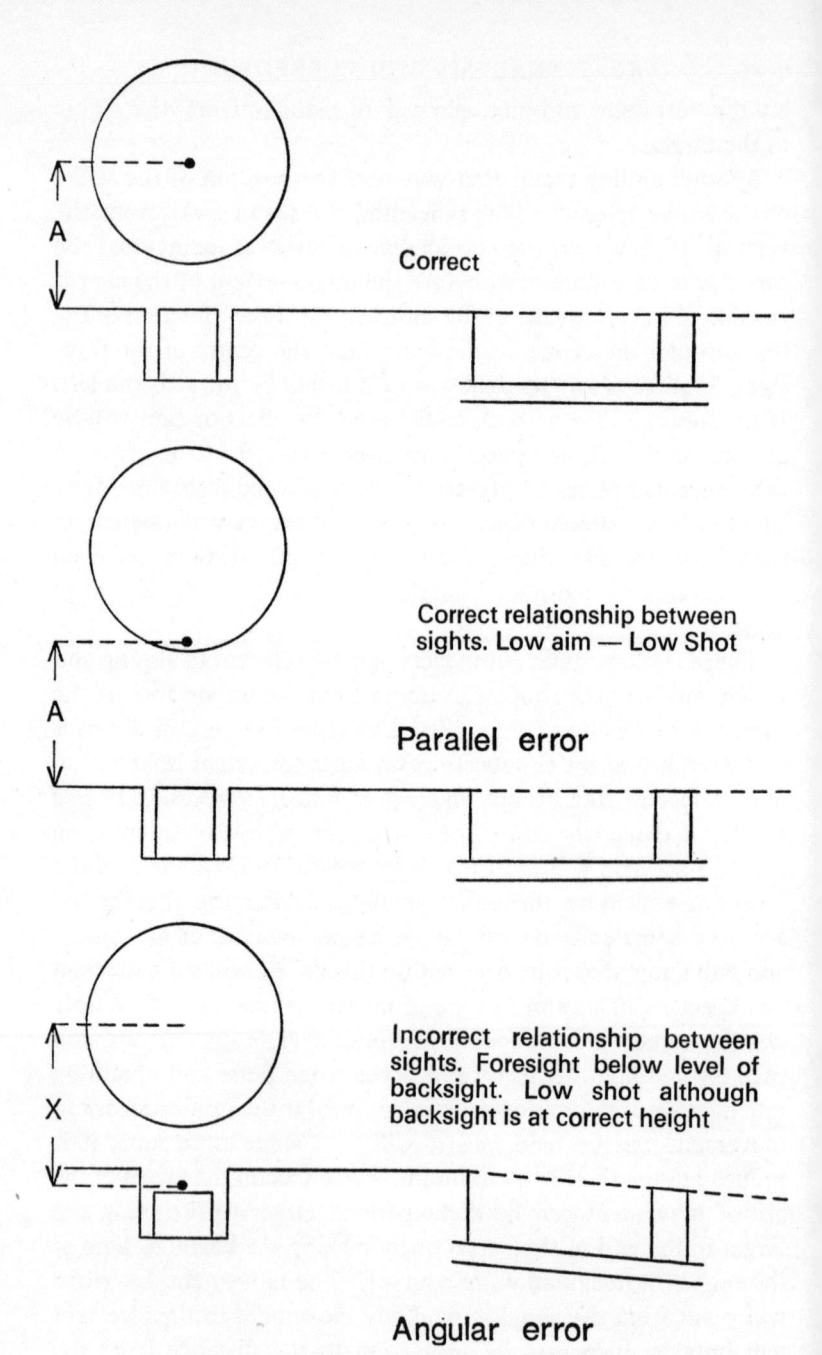

15. *Relation between parallel and angular errors*

FAULT ANALYSIS AND CORRECTION

shoulder to the foresight in relation to the distance of the range. A movement of $\frac{1}{100}$ inch by the foresight will only produce a $\frac{1}{2}$ inch circle on the target at 50 yards and any good shooter should be able to control his gun so as to limit the movement to that extent. This does not mean that a good shooter will be able to group to $\frac{1}{2}$ inch at 50 yards but that he should be able to hold his pistol still enough to limit the arc of movement to this extent.

On the other hand, if the sight relationship is incorrect the same error of $\frac{1}{100}$ inch will produce a 3 inch error at 50 yards.

The errors produced by arc of movement are parallel errors and errors of displacement are angular errors.

It should now be obvious that it is important to get the correct relation between the foresight and the backsight. Errors in this relation, being angular, will show a greater deflection on the target as the range increases. Errors in placing the correct sight picture against the target will be in exact relationship to the position of the aim on the target. The importance of the correct aim will be repeated on several occasions in this book as it does not matter how much trouble the shooter has taken in preparing for the shot if he takes a poor aim. A poor aim will produce a poor shot and all the effort will be wasted. On the other hand if the shooter makes mistakes in other aspects of firing the shot but takes a good aim, the shot is unlikely to be a poor one—it may not be a perfect one but it should be a good one.

If the shooter finds that he is having difficulty in holding the aim he should first check his stance. If the stance is incorrect he will be off balance and will have to strain his muscles to hold the pistol on the correct line. As he comes to the end of the shoot he may find that the arm is taking up the line of the natural aim at the moment of firing. The remedy is easy and that is to make sure by trial aim that the shooter does have the right stance. This can be checked as often as the shooter wishes.

Faulty holding of the grip will show either in displacement of the odd shot or in a complete shift of the group. The grip should be made so that the shooter can only hold it one way, any other way will feel wrong. If the grip is held too loosely then the weight of the gun will tend to fall against the open side of the hand and

FAULT ANALYSIS AND CORRECTION

in a right-handed shooter this will cause the barrel to point low and left. The aim may appear to be correct but the recoil of the gun at the moment of firing will force the gun towards the point of least resistance and so throw the shot low and left. If the grip is too tight then the heel of the hand will push against the bottom of the grip and tend to push the gun to the right and slightly upwards. The recoil of the gun will cause the shots to go in that direction. If the gun is held very tightly then the hand will become tired, pulse movements will be communicated to the gun and it will be impossible to hold the pistol still.

Faults in holding the grip will be overcome with practice. Firstly, it must be held the same way for each shot and, secondly, it must be held with a positive grip. This is to say that as much of the surface of the hand must be in contact with the grip and held firmly enough for the hand to feel that it is holding the pistol. The usual way of taking the grip is to pick up the pistol barrel with an overhand grip in the left hand (making sure that the hand does not cover the muzzle); then the right hand is pushed against the grip and the fingers curled round the front of the grip. This method helps to make sure that as much of the hand is in touch with the grip before the grip has to support the gun.

Incorrect trigger technique will account for loss of quite a number of points. If the trigger is not let off smoothly or progressively then the shot is unlikely to be a good one. Set Trigger technique is discussed in the chapter concerned with Free Pistol shooting.

Ideally the trigger should be released when the sight picture is correct but if the trigger is jerked off at this point then the sudden action will be transmitted to the whole of the gun and a bad shot will appear on the target either low right or low left. The centre of gravity of the pistol is in the area of the trigger and sudden movement in this vicinity will bring the pistol off centre. The direction of the shot will depend upon the way the shooter snatches or jerks the trigger. If the trigger is pulled with the pad of the forefinger on the side of the trigger then the pistol will tend to be directed to the side on which the pressure is being applied,

FAULT ANALYSIS AND CORRECTION

and also low. If the shooter finds that he is getting such shots he must examine his trigger release to ensure that the pad of the finger is falling directly on to the lower part of the trigger and that the trigger is being pulled directly to the rear along the axis of the pistol.

There is another common fault which involves trigger release. Having brought the pistol on aim most shooters try to get the shot off first time. Some will persist in the aim until it is fired taking perhaps more than fifteen seconds over the shot. Then in a last despairing effort the shot is fired when the shooter thinks he has the correct aim. The shot is nowhere near the declared point of aim and the shooter blames every other cause than taking too long over the shot. The main reason for holding on too long is lack of confidence in the shooter's own ability and the fear of firing a bad shot. The shot must be fired within a reasonable time before the shooter begins to tire and although the shooter may not feel himself getting tired, he cannot concentrate fully for more than seven to eight seconds. He does, however, if he plans his shooting, have plenty of time for each shot, plenty of time to take a progressive trigger release.

Jerking and snatching the trigger is mainly a problem for the beginner, especially when using noisy full-bore pistols. The shooter wants to get the shot in the middle of the target and he has not yet reached the stage of holding the pistol reasonably still. He will try to get the shot off as the foresight is passing the centre of the target. At the same time he will be anticipating the recoil and will push forward with his arm to counteract it. Anything can happen to such shots and the shooter will be disappointed. It is very important that the learner is taught not to jerk the trigger, because if it does become a habit it is hard to eradicate. The best way to overcome snatching is plenty of dry practice concentrating on trigger control. By constant training the beginner will not only learn instinctive trigger control, but at the same time will condition the muscles to control the pistol whilst on aim to avoid the anticipation of the recoil. A good instructor should be able to spot a shooter who develops anticipation of recoil, or 'flinch', and will take him off live shooting to

FAULT ANALYSIS AND CORRECTION

rectify the fault. The fault will show in an experienced shooter by a vertically elongated group with low shots.

If a shooter is suspected of snatching the trigger or flinching, the fault can be demonstrated with an assistant. Dummy cartridges are introduced without the knowledge of the shooter. The faults of the shooter will be obvious when he comes to fire the dummy. This method of demonstrating must be very carefully controlled from the safety angle.

It has been shown that the shooter can be subject to various faults in technique but that all can be remedied by practice in the correct methods. However, there will be unexplained shots away from the declared aim over which the shooter has no control. These are caused by muscular tremors which can be exaggerated under stress into 'twitches'. Muscular tremors are present in all muscular movement. They are very small and will probably account in a small way for the arc of movement in the pistol when on aim. When the shooter is under stress, as can occur in a big match, the muscular tremors can build up into a spasm. If this happens when the shooter is in the process of firing and has committed himself to the shot there is nothing he can do and the shot will be off centre. The spasm cannot be controlled. It is not known at present why these spasms occur and research is being undertaken in the field of manual control systems where muscular movements have to be transmitted through mechanical systems with very small tolerances. It is postulated that all muscular movements are the result of electrical discharges within the muscle cells. If an electrical potential builds up without being gradually dissipated it will suddenly discharge and cause an involuntary twitch.

Thus an examination of the art of pistol shooting shows the involvement of neurological and, as will be seen later, of psychological factors.

8

Physical Condition

It is impossible for a shooter to maintain a high performance if he is not in good physical condition. This does not mean that top shooters are muscle bound or capable of running a mile in four minutes. There must be moderation in everything. The shooter should be in such condition that he can maintain his performance over the whole period of the shoot. This means that the stamina required must be built up by selective exercise. The breathing capacity must be sufficiently developed to supply the blood to the extremities with adequate amounts of oxygen whilst the breathing is restrained and the system should be trained to co-ordinate its muscular activity and react quickly to external stimuli.

Fundamentally the whole system requires all-round physical development as there are few parts of the body that are not put to use during pistol shooting. The body has to adopt an almost upright stance with the weight of the trunk supported by the backbone and this weight transferred through the legs to the ground. The body has to be kept as still as possible and both abdominal and back muscles are brought into play for this.

The arm has to hold a weight at its extremity as still as possible. The arm muscles will hold this weight in a complex manner with much of the weight of the arm transferred through the shoulder muscles to the back. These muscles must be flexible to respond to minute changes in position of the pistol and to bring the pistol into the right position. If any of the muscles are out of condition they will be unable to co-ordinate readily with other muscles and holding an aim will prove difficult and tiring. It

PHYSICAL CONDITION

naturally follows that it is unwise to expect good scores if one goes on the range tired, or having recently taken heavy exercise.

Pistol shooting caters for people of all ages and age is compensated for by experience. The vigorous exercise that can be indulged in by youth is not at all suitable for those getting on in years, but many shooters can maintain a high performance over many years. Torsten Ullman of Sweden appeared on the international scene in the 1936 Olympic Games where he won a gold medal. He was still in the top flight when he competed in the Rome Olympics in 1960 and would probably have continued his international career much longer but for an unfortunate accident to his trigger finger. There cannot be many sports where youth can compete with age on equal terms and where efficiency can continue and even improve over a long time.

Shooting is not confined to a particular season of the year although there are times when important competitions are staged. The major national competitions are usually held at the same time each year, but international competitions are held at the time most suitable for the host nation. The shooter must therefore keep himself in good condition all the time and take a little extra care in training when the big match approaches. Special exercises have been developed for the muscles that will be most concerned and these exercises can be used for group or individual training. They are reproduced in the Appendix by kind permission of the Commanding Officer, United States Army Advanced Marksmanship Training Unit.

The shooter should be in normal good health and take a reasonable amount of exercise. Walking is very good for the whole system as not only does it give the participant plenty of fresh air, but it virtually uses all the muscles in the body, especially if it is done in hilly areas. Swimming is an excellent way of using the body muscles and it is particularly good for strengthening the lungs. Swimming as a method of training should be kept to those parts of the season which are relatively unimportant for shooting, but as relaxation swimming is useful at any time.

A shooter need not confine himself to shooting as his sole form of sport, and participation in a more vigorous one will keep the shooter fit without his having to undertake any special training. Tennis, squash, golf, badminton can give plenty of exercise and strengthen the muscles used by the shooter. But such sport, apart from golf, should be given a rest when serious shooting training reaches its climax, for exercise should be interspersed with periods of rest and it is just as vital for the shooter to have sufficient rest for him to have sufficient exercise. It is easy to sit up half the night talking to friends about shooting problems, but the shooter would be far better asleep in bed!

Strengthening exercises can be very simple. The lifting and holding of the pistol can be simulated by using a milk bottle filled with water to the necessary weight or by holding a smoothing iron at arm's length. Some shooters hold a stick with a weight hanging on the end. Squeezing a rubber ball will strengthen the muscles in the hand, but just forcing the fingers right out and then clenching the hand under tension will be sufficient. Just try doing this five times in succession and the hand will feel the exercise. No exercises should be carried to extremes, as injury can occur. If muscles or ligaments do become strained then proper medical attention should be sought.

Shooting involves short periods of intense concentration alternating with periods of relaxation. General exercises can build up stamina but the specific exercises should be short and dynamic. These short and sharp exercises must be started gently but built up in number as the shooter grows more proficient. Stop when the effort is felt, but next time or the time after it will be possible to try one or two more.

Exercise means the consumption of energy and the good shooter will watch his diet to see that when training he has body-building foods. During shooting he should take the food that suits him best at that time. Diet is very much a matter of common sense but some basic principles should be laid down. It is generally unwise to shoot on an empty stomach just as it is unwise to work on an empty stomach. The body will feel weak and as time passes the lack of food will be felt both physically and mentally. A light meal should be taken not later than one hour

PHYSICAL CONDITION

before the match and this should be a high energy content meal of small bulk. The stomach feels more comfortable with food inside but it will not need to be overloaded and so impose a strain on the digestion. The digestive system needs a lot of oxygenated blood to cope with a large meal, but the shooter needs the oxygen in the brain not in his stomach! This means easily digested foods. It is unwise to experiment with foods at this stage, stick to foods the reaction to which is known. Try the new ones after shooting has finished and the immediate consequences do not matter. After having the light meal before the match, the shooter should relax quietly until the time of the match.

If the shooting is prolonged then the shooter might find the need for intermediate refreshment. There are many sources of quick energy ranging from glucose or even plain sugar cubes to fruit juice. Liquids should be taken with the chill off. The shooter will find for himself the best form of sugar intake, but the most popular is boiled sweets or hard candy.

It is inadvisable to use alcohol on the range as a stimulant. Everybody knows that alcohol gives a feeling of well-being and confidence, but even the smallest amount will alter reaction times and affect the co-ordination of eye and muscle. People do drink before and during friendly matches but on the big occasion alcohol should on no account be taken.

Smoking is also detrimental to good shooting. A great number of shooters smoke, even during a shoot, but amongst the better shooters there will be a greater proportion who do not smoke. Smoking is detrimental to breathing and will increase the pulse. The average shooter who likes to smoke should try an experiment to show the effect on his shooting. Refrain from smoking until the first card has been fired, then have a cigarette and immediately fire another card. The difference in the two cards should be quite apparent. Rest for fifteen minutes and fire another card; although this will be better than the second one it will still not be of the same standard as the first. It will take quite some time for the breathing and pulse to return to normal. If smoking is necessary, then it should be indulged in with moderation but reduced to a minimum before the big match and not done at all during the

PHYSICAL CONDITION

match. The best advice is to stop smoking altogether and use the money to buy more ammunition or better equipment.

The taking of drugs and stimulants is of no help at all to the shooter. Experiments have been tried using mild forms of tranquillizers and although the firer seems to himself to be in first-class condition, the co-ordination required to maintain a high standard is impossible to achieve. Any drugs have an affect on co-ordination and even apparently harmless ones like aspirin can affect the shooter's reactions. Before important matches nervous tension can build up overnight and the shooter might feel inclined to take a sleeping pill to get a good night's rest. This could have a deleterious effect next morning. The shooter would do better to have a walk, shower and a warm drink before going to bed to encourage natural sleep.

Physical aspects of shooting will include care of the body as well as its training. The right sort of clothing, that fits where it should and is loose where it needs to be, and footwear that does not cramp the feet are minor points but are important if they enable the shooter to really feel right when he is on the range. Another point that will help the shooter is to see that he has towelling or tissue to keep his hands and face free from perspiration when shooting in hot weather. He should not forget the salt tablets in these conditions to counteract the loss of salt from his body by heavy perspiration. Little points but all are morale boosting.

Care must be taken of the eyes, as they undergo considerable strain during a prolonged shoot. When the eye is at rest it will be focused at infinity and it takes a conscious effort to focus objects. If the shooter switches his focus from object to object, that is from foresight to target and back at frequent intervals, he will be subjecting the eye muscles to unnecessary strain and the eye will feel tired. Blinking is a natural function, but has to be controlled during aiming and firing. After the shot has been fired, the eyes must blink. This relaxes the eye muscles, and allows the fluid on the surface of the eyeball to circulate, cleaning and refreshing it. Sometimes the eye feels dry and irritated. To relieve this, most shooters keep in their shooting box a small bottle of eye fluid which can be dropped into the eye. This does no harm and can be used, if required, in the middle of a shoot. It is refreshing and beneficial to the comfort of the eye.

The eye should be rested between shots as much as possible. This can be done either by closing the eyes and relaxing the eye muscles or by looking at a restful colour without trying to focus the eyes. Green is probably the best colour and a shady patch of grass outside the firing point is a good place to look at.

Eye defects should receive proper attention at the earliest possible moment. Most eye defects can be rectified and, if necessary, glasses can be prescribed to enable the shooter to see his foresight in perfect focus even though without glasses he is unable to do so.

Ears must be protected. It has been found that many shooters in the past suffered from high-frequency deafness caused by damage to the nerve cells of the ear. When such nerve cells are damaged they do not recover and damage is progressive the more the ear is exposed to excessive noise. The report of a ·38 or ·45 is shattering in an enclosed area, but the effect of a ·22 is just as damaging over a long period. Although slight damage will cause only high-frequency loss, progressive damage can occur and the shooter becomes recognizably deaf. A hearing aid in these circumstances will be of no benefit.

The December 1966 issue of *The Rifleman* contains a report of an investigation organized for the N.S.R.A. by the Audiology Group of the Institute of Sound and Vibration Research at the University of Southampton on the effect of shooting as a hazard to hearing. The investigation was carried out using ·22 rifles and the conclusion reached was that there is some risk of slight hearing damage occurring in noise-sensitive individuals from indoor firing of the ·22 rifle. The final paragraph of the report is the most important and is quoted in full. The italics are mine.

'Unfortunately, the range used for the audiometric investigation was not licensed for pistol shooting, but the report from a ·22 pistol was measured on the outdoor range. The peak pressure level measured two feet to one side of the muzzle was found to be 153 decibels compared with 139 decibels from a rifle fired under

PHYSICAL CONDITION

similar conditions. *This corresponds to a peak pressure level about five times as great.*

'The pressure at the ear is also greater, the right ear being more likely to be affected in pistol shooting. Ear protection should always be worn whilst firing pistols indoors.'

There are two kinds of ear protectors, internal and external. Internal are either properly fitted ear moulds incorporating sound filters, or soft rubber plugs with filters. It is of no benefit at all to use empty cartridge cases or cotton wool as these do not filter out the dangerous shock waves. Internal protectors must be kept clean so that the ear does not become infected. External ear muffs are being made in large quantities for commercial use as many industrial undertakings are providing their employees with this kind of protection. One has only to think of people working in close proximity to jet aircraft to realize the need. It is probable that the noise intensity of an aircraft engine is no greater, taking into account the time factor, than the report of a shot. Special models are produced for shooters which give excellent protection and are comfortable to wear. If the ears are very sensitive it is possible to wear external muffs over the internal protectors.

Protectors do not cut out all sound and they still allow the shooter to hear the instructions of the range officer. They do help to cut out the sounds of conversation and help the shooter to concentrate on his shooting. He will not be disturbed by the noise of firing from neighbouring shooters. A sudden noise close to a shooter's ear can have disastrous consequences if he is using a free pistol. Many shots have been fired involuntarily as a result.

By taking reasonable care with training and physical well-being the shooter will be able to raise his scores and maintain his shooting efficiency at a high level.

The aerobic method is recommended for achieving and maintaining fitness. This is described in *The New Aerobics* by K. H. Cooper (Bantam Books). It is a general method which by planned exertion will improve the efficiency of the body processes.

Before following a physical training programme which will involve strenuous exertion it is wise to have a medical check-up and to visit an oculist regularly.

9

The Mental Approach

This chapter will deal with the attitude of mind which a successful shooter must develop if he is to give a top-class performance under any conditions. The shooter may have mastered the techniques, but unless he has the right mental approach he will never succeed.

The shooter must adopt a positive approach to his performance. Whatever level of performance the shooter has achieved, it should follow that under the same conditions he should be able to repeat that performance. This does not always happen and it is probably due to the mental approach rather than bad technique. He cannot, however, reasonably expect his ultimate score to be way above his normal average. The most that he can expect is that it should be within the upper bracket of the scores that go to make up his average.

The positive attitude can be developed by having confidence in one's own ability. When planning the shot, the shooter must go through in his mind the technique for scoring a good shot. The mind must keep control over these processes and not allow any slackness. The positive attitude should be: 'There is no reason why this should not be a good shot, it should be a good shot, it WILL be a good shot' and by concentrating hard in this frame of mind, it will be a good shot.

Shooters are, however, only human and cannot work like machines. There will be times when the shoot is not going quite the way hoped for and negative thoughts will come into the mind to interfere with the mental discipline. It is easy to say that the range is poor, the light is bad, the shooter is not as good as the other competitors, etc. If these thoughts do enter the mind they must be changed to positive thinking, the range may be poor and the light may be bad, but they are the same for the other shooters and if they succumb, then this is the opportunity to concentrate harder to ignore the conditions. It has often been found that a shooter will do better when the conditions are a bit rough because he will really concentrate with determination to overcome them. Other competitors should never be the concern of a shooter on the range. On the range and in a match the shooter has no friends, unless he is shooting in a team. The other shooters are no better; they have probably never shot a highest possible score, they are probably having the same kind of thoughts and trying to eradicate them from their minds. Ignore the others and concentrate on your own shooting, knowing that there is no reason at all why the score should not be a record and win the match.

But one must be on guard against carelessness and over-confidence. After a string of good shots, one can think: 'This is easy.' Over-confidence creeps in and carelessness results. Every shot must be worked for and the shooter must never shoot down to a score.

The average shooter will want to take an interest in what is going on around him during a shoot. It is natural to want to find out what the other shooters are scoring, particularly if he himself is doing well, and the easiest way is to look at their targets through the telescope. When doing this it is more natural to look at the shots in the middle and miss those on the outside and so a false impression is obtained of the other shooters' ability. Avoid looking at other people's targets; it will not help any shooter to do better and is distracting and demoralizing. The only use for the telescope is to have a quick look at one's own target to check the position of the shot. The shot has been fired and whatever the score, it cannot be changed. Therefore it is not the slightest use worrying about the score, or adding it up as the shoot progresses. This will only alter the score of the remaining shots in a downwards direction. If the shoot is not going too well, then a running total will be depressing. If it is going well and a record score is in sight, then this may make the shooter nervous and spoil his chance. Whatever the previous shot, the next one is separate and before it is fired it is a potential 'X'. There is no reason why it should not be an 'X'.

It has been said that the hardest part of shooting is not the actual firing of the shot but the interval between shots. In slow fire there is plenty of time between shots and the normal rate of fire in standard N.S.R.A. competitions is one shot per minute. The actual firing from the time the pistol is lifted up to the release of the shot should not be more than fifteen seconds. The shooter has ample time to have more than one attempt at firing each shot to make sure that he gets the best possible shot. If he does fire the shot at the first attempt then he has at least forty-five seconds to relax between each shot. Although the shooter in this time will spot the shot and analyse the reason for its placing on the target, it must be an interval of relaxation. In a long shoot such as the 60 shot U.I.T. Free Pistol match the relaxation must be positive and the shooter will be able to sit down and take his mind off shooting for a short while. He might like to read a paper or book to give the mind a change so that when the next shot is fired it is refreshed. Some shooters relax by leaving the firing point for a short walk.

Every shooter has an upper level of achievement, but this should not prevent him from reaching this level when required to do so. It is doubtful whether any shooter really knows his upper level as this can only be found by long training, but he will know his normal top level. Not every shooter can reach top international class, but whatever level the shooter achieves he must be determined to do his best. It is well known that some shooters get very good scores when shooting on their own range or in practice, but when having to shoot on other ranges or in matches are unable to reproduce their form. This is the inability to cope with match pressure. Match pressure is felt by all shooters whether shooting at club level or at international level. The shooters who win are those who have managed, by exercising mental discipline, to convert match pressure to their advantage.

By examining the negative attitude towards match pressure the

19. Free Pistol. A very natural stance. (H. Cullum)

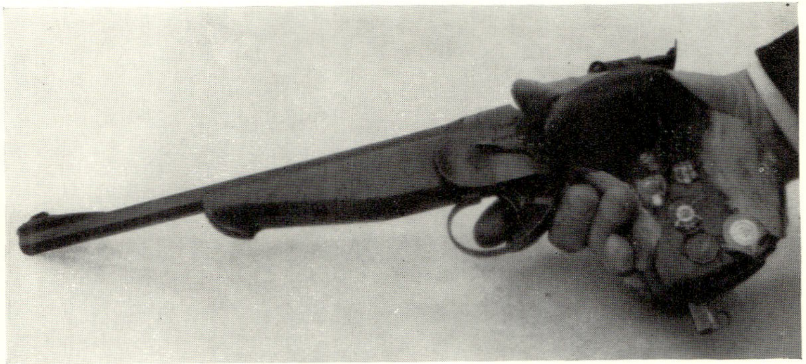

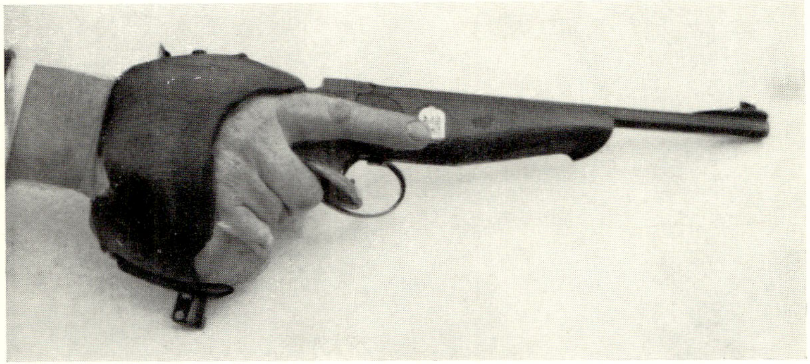

20 and 21. Free Pistol Grip. Fingers well supported. Grip clear of wrist joint. Forefinger quite free.

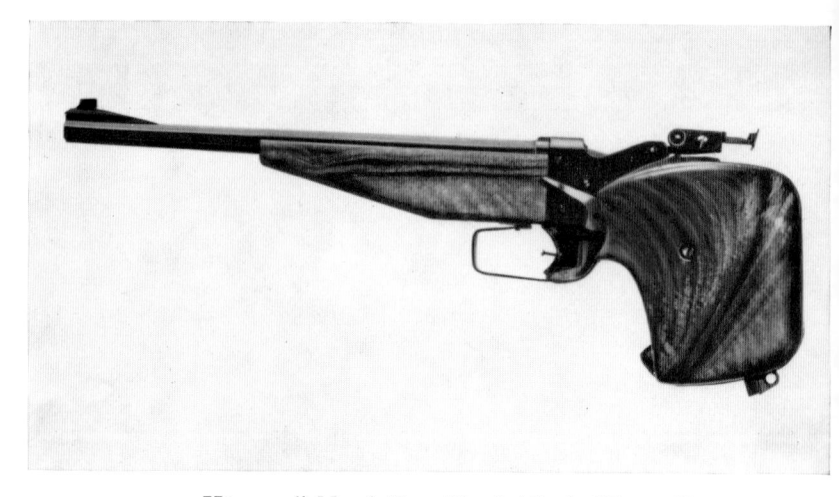

22. Hämmerli Match Free Pistol. (*S. A. Hämmerli*)

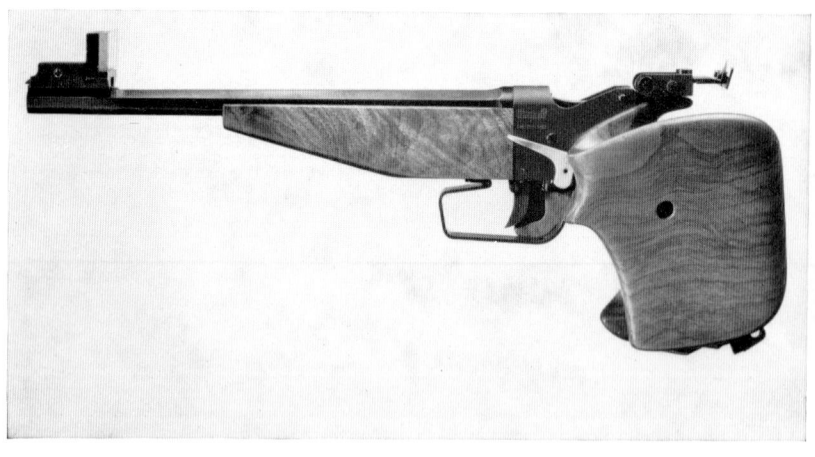

23. Hämmerli Match Pistol fitted with mirror sights. (*S. A. Hämmerli*)

kind of problems that have to be overcome can be seen. The first premise is that the shooter has the ability to win the match but is unable to reproduce his best form. This arises from the fear that he will not shoot well and that he cannot win. He fears such failure and his score will show up in a bad light against his previous record. This fear will show in his inability to hold the gun steady and to concentrate. He will become trigger shy as he feels that if he fires it will be a bad shot. This fear of the bad shot imposes itself over the whole of his shoot and he will be unable to co-ordinate his techniques. He will come up on aim time and time again in an attempt to fire. In the end the shooter finds that he is running short of time and will have to force himself to fire. He will then probably start to shoot better but will have left it too late to make a good recovery.

These negative attitudes can be overcome but it will take time and patience. It is quite likely that the first time a shooter shoots in a match big or small, his score will be under his average. He will have to learn by experience and the example of others that match pressure can be overcome. He must have the determination to overcome it. This is the first positive step: determination to succeed, determination to conquer the butterflies in the stomach. Much of the nervousness is due to glandular excretion which upsets and excites the system. If the shooter can control the excitement then the extra nervous energy released can be put to good advantage. The eye will appear to see better, the concentration will be deeper and reaction time quickened. Under normal conditions reaction time between seeing and doing is about one-fifth of a second, when trained this will speed up to about one-tenth of a second and under match pressure to perhaps one-twentieth of a second.

The second positive approach is the planning of the shot. The previous shot must be analysed and the reason for its position on the target ascertained. The error, if any, must be mentally rectified so that the next shot can be better. If the previous shot was a bad one, the shooter must not dwell on that fact, but on the fact that the previous shot was an isolated incident in a series and the reason for its position is known. If the previous shot was a good one, then the shooter will remember exactly how it was fired so that he can fire the next one in exactly the same way.

The third positive step is to be confident in one's own ability. This is something that the shooter knows. He must appear confident not only to himself, but to the other shooters so that he can gain some moral advantage. The negative attitude opposed to this is that of the shooter who gets upset when he has a bad shot and says so in no uncertain terms. The shooter must remain as calm as possible as this will help him to relax between shots and so conserve his energies for the few vital seconds connected with the release of a shot.

So far the arguments have been general but they should be applied in particular. The novice should have no inhibitions and his mental approach will be very straightforward. He will know that he has no particular standard and will spend his odd moments on the range examining, learning and practising the techniques. He should, however, be started fairly early to fire to a standard so that he can measure his progress. This can be done by firing match cards to obtain certain scores and he will feel some sort of pressure if he has to finish a shoot with upwards from a seven to reach his standard.

The novice will, as he progresses, begin to take part in club teams and open individual competitions and will develop a match temperament. The progress is gradual and he must expect to have some upsets, but if he expects these then it will do no harm. By this gradual progress and with a positive approach the shooter will learn to apply the correct techniques in any situation. It can be dangerous if an untried shooter is selected for a match. The shooter may fail to come up to expectations and may always have this failure on his mind on future occasions. The selection of the untried shooter must only be done after consideration of all the factors involved, not least being the effect on the shooter.

It should be realized that every shooter has to undergo match pressure before he can overcome it and succeed. Two illustrations of match pressure come to mind. Torsten Ullman was shooting in the 1959 European Championships in Milan and was involved

THE MENTAL APPROACH

in some dispute. The manager of his team took over the problem and after long arguments it was satisfactorily settled. All this time Ullman was settled in his chair patiently waiting to resume shooting. Time was passing as well but this did not seem to worry him. When the dispute had been settled and extension of time allowed, he was asked to continue his shoot. He did a couple of 'knees bend', took a few deep breaths and continued as if nothing had happened. He scored 552 points to take fourth place in the Free Pistol.

The other illustration concerns the author when shooting in the British Championship in 1954. The final resulted in a tie and under the N.S.R.A. rules a tie shoot was required. This involved another ten shots with only the two shooters on the range. At that time the author did not have a great deal of experience with the pistol and the strain was heavy. In spite of this he managed to concentrate better than his opponent and won the match. At the end, a spectator took his pulse and found it to register 116, against the normal rate of 72.

Those who have the opportunity to watch experienced shooters will be aware of their detachment whilst they are shooting. This will go when they have finished shooting but it is unwise and unfair to approach them before or during a shoot as they will be giving their whole effort to the shoot. There are, of course, the exceptions who like somebody to talk to, but do not approach the shooter, let him approach you. After he has finished he will want to relax and will be found to be the best of company.

10

The Free Pistol

Slow-fire shooting with standard pistols is not the only form of pistol shooting for which there are recognized competitions. For small bore there are in addition timed and rapid fire at 20 yards, silhouette shooting at 25 metres and Free Pistol at 50 metres. There are also various competitions for centre-fire pistols. It is proposed to take each of these types of shooting in turn and examine how the fundamental techniques are adapted to suit the particular competition.

The 50 metres Free Pistol shoot is one of the major pistol events in the most important international competitions such as Olympic Games, World and Regional Championships. The target is a white square with circular scoring rings with a central 10 ring 5 centimetres (2 inches) in diameter and an outside ring of 50 centimetres (20 inches). Each ring from the centre increases in diameter by 5 centimetres whilst the score decreases by 1 point from 10 to 1. The aiming mark is black and covers the 7 ring which is 20 centimetres (8 inches) in diameter. The competition is of 60 shots, which together with 15 sighting shots is fired in a maximum time of two and a half hours. It is a gruelling shoot and is rightly known as the classic pistol match.

Any ·22 target pistol can be used in these matches but the majority of shooters will use a free pistol. Free pistols or match pistols are designed for this type of target shooting and have been developed to a very fine art over many years. They are very fine examples of the gunmaker's art and are precision built. They are very accurate and have a very light 'set' or 'hair' trigger so

THE FREE PISTOL

that very little effort is needed to release it. Of post-war manufacture the best known are the Swiss Hämmerli and the Russian Mu & Toz, though the pre-war Anschutz free pistol is still in common use.

The fundamental difference between a free pistol and other types is in the trigger mechanism. The free pistol trigger can be set to any weight to suit the shooter's own requirement. It can be set so delicately that if the pistol is raised with the barrel in an upright position the trigger will be released under its own weight without being touched. Most shooters find a trigger weight of about 10–15 grams is satisfactory.

The fundamental principle of a free trigger is that after being cocked the spring operating the trigger is pre-set by a lever. This pre-setting requires the force of about 1 kilogram and this force is stored in bent leaf springs and can be released by the touch of the trigger. Various free pistols have different designs of action and trigger mechanisms and it would be difficult to describe them all in detail in this volume. The shooter should, however, make himself familiar with the mechanism, not only with its parts but with the way it functions. As these pistols are precision engineered their adjustment is the work of skilled mechanics and the amateur enthusiast can do irreparable harm if he attempts internal adjustments or repairs without complete and proper knowledge or skill.

There are some points that should be considered in the care and maintenance of free pistols. Both the barrel and the mechanism should be kept very clean. This is not contrary to what has just been said about repairs. It is quite feasible to dismantle the main parts of the mechanism for cleaning but it helps to avoid frequent dismantling of the pistol if the ammunition is cleaned of excess grease or lubricant as it is this grease that combines with dirt and fouling and clogs the mechanism. This can be removed from the ammunition by wiping each round gently with a soft cloth, and from the mechanism by using a soft blunt tool. The ubiquitous matchstick is a most useful tool for getting into awkward corners. Do not use too much lubricant and remember that *oil must be kept away from delicate trigger mechanisms*. Particularly in the case of the Hämmerli, the trigger mechanism's multiple springs must be kept dry. The usual way of degreasing mechanisms is to use a grease-free spirit and then let the parts dry out by themselves whilst keeping them protected from dust. If trigger springs become oily then they are likely to slip and a premature discharge can take place.

These pistols are expensive and should be well cared for; as by their very nature repairs are also expensive. Repairs can be avoided if good care is taken of the pistol and if parts are replaced as soon as inspection shows that this is necessary. It is better to replace a part before a match than risk a failure in the match which could be disastrous. Before any big match it is wise to have the pistol overhauled by a competent armourer. It is also wise to carry spares for those parts which could give trouble so that in an emergency a part may be changed on the spot. Armourers or expert amateurs will usually be found at any large meeting.

Although commercial free pistols operate mechanically developments are being made with electrically operated pistols. The pistol is loaded and cocked mechanically but the trigger release is electrically operated. All that is then needed to fire the pistol is a touch of a micro-switch which can be set to any desired pressure. As there is no mechanical linkage between the trigger and the mechanism of the pistol, only an electrical one, the grip can be set in any position under the barrel. It may be that in time commercial weapons will develop along these lines.

Free pistols are very accurate and test groups will be expected to be much less than $\frac{1}{2}$ inch at 50 metres. The gun and ammunition will group much closer than the shooter will ever be able to group and it is this fact that must give the shooter complete confidence in his pistol. He knows that if he shoots straight, the shot will go into the 10 ring. The official world record for the free pistol match is 566 ex 600 (A. Jassinky, U.S.S.R., in Bucharest, 1955). This leaves ample room for improvement but gives some indication of the difficulty of reaching a really high score under match conditions. Higher scores than this have been fired in practice and in matches not qualifying for recognition as world records. But this high score means that the shooter must

THE FREE PISTOL

have fired a group, except possibly for one or two shots, of a diameter of about 10 centimetres (less than 4 inches).

The free pistol is usually heavier than the standard pistol and the shooter must in the first place learn to hold this heavier weight quite still. The right shape of grip is therefore of vital importance. The details of making a grip have been described in a previous chapter but very great care must be taken with these grips. It is essential that the grip is fitted to the gun at the right angle to suit the shooter. The pistol is usually barrel heavy so that when the arm is raised the weight of the pistol causes the wrist to drop forward at an angle to the forearm. As the forearm has to be raised above the shoulder level to bring the pistol up to the line of sight the hand is not at such an angle with the line of fire as at first thought. It is this angle that must be considered when fitting the grips to the pistol and a certain amount of experiment will be required to get this angle correct for the shooter. When it is correct the grip will feel comfortable and the pistol when raised will be very close to the natural line of sight. The less the amount the pistol has to be moved in the aim to bring it into the line of sight the less will be the strain on the shooter's muscles.

As the free pistol grip will be a very close fit to the hand it must be borne in mind that the size of the hand will change with temperature. If it is warm then the hand will be full of blood circulating close to the skin; it will then appear to be fatter and will be a tighter fit in the grip. In the cold weather, however, the capillaries in the skin contract and there is not so much blood in the hand. The grip will then feel looser. Most grips have an adjustable hand support which can be raised or lowered and this will allow for expansion or contraction in the hand. The perfect fitting grip should be made for the most likely conditions rather than for the average. The hands should always be wiped with a towel or absorbent tissue before picking up the grip as the moisture on the surface of the skin may let the hand slide within the grip. If this tends to occur despite the precautionary measures mentioned, a dusting of powdered rosin will help.

THE FREE PISTOL

The shooter will find by experiment which type of sights suits him best. The foresight will be a blade, but this can be made in various widths, some shooters like a narrow blade and others prefer a wide one. Backsights are wide to allow the shooter to get a very good level line across the target. The notch in the backsight may be either semicircular or square. The square ones are more commonly used as this type enables the vertical sides of the foresight to be more accurately positioned in the notch. What is important here is that there should be sufficient light on either side of the foresight when viewed through the backsight. There must be sufficient light for the eye to be able to balance one side against the other. If the width of the foresight is changed then a comparable change must be made with the backsight notch. It could be argued that the perfect sight would be when the foresight exactly filled the backsight notch, i.e. when the firer could see no light on either side of the foresight it must be in the middle of the backsight. This would not be possible in practice as in the first place the pistol could not be held steady enough and in the second place there would be no mark for the eye to centre the sights on the target. To do this both sides of the foresight must be visible.

Shooters experiment with sights and various modifications will be seen at any large competition. The most common modification will be to build up the height of the sights above the line of the barrel so that the gun does not have to be raised above the height of the shoulder. This imposes less strain on the muscles. When such a modification is made it must be remembered that the greater the distance between the muzzle and the line of sight the greater will be any error on the target whether angular or parallel. For instance if the gun is canted the arc of movement is directly related to this distance. Other shooters extend the sight base, here the difficulty is in holding the aim as the longer the sight base the greater will be the apparent movement of the foresight.

The mirror sight has been introduced to free pistol shooting by Reiny Ruess, a member of the Swiss National Team. It is described in the March 1967 edition of *Hämmerli News* and the following description is adapted from this bulletin. The foresight is substituted by a parabolic mirror with a focal length of the distance between the mirror and the backsight. The conventional backsight is substituted by a small plate which is white on the

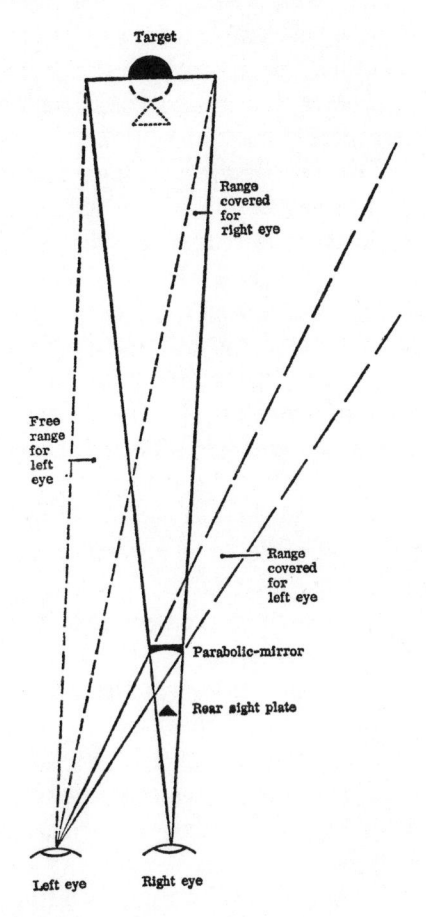

16. *Sighting process when using mirror sights*

target side with a black triangle whose apex is just below the centre of the plate. This triangle is reflected in the mirror and because the mirror is parabolic the focus to the eye of the reflected triangle is at infinity. The target is also at infinity to the eye.

THE FREE PISTOL

The eye can then focus on the target and the reflected sight at the same time. The backsight plate must be well illuminated and this sight is not suitable for indoor ranges.

The method of aiming is to bring the pistol into the aiming position and let the mirror cover the lower half of the aiming mark. Close the aiming eye and focus the other eye on the target. The aiming eye is then opened and the triangle will be seen in the mirror. The shooter then brings the triangle into the right position under the aiming mark and fires.

This method of aiming has the advantage that the eye is used in its most relaxed focus. Both eyes are open and conventional shooting glasses are not required. As the shooter grows older he finds that it becomes harder to focus at short distances and therefore this method will appeal to him.

These sights are now not approved for use in competitions under U.I.T. Regulations. The diagram (16) shows the sighting process.

The part of the pistol which really distinguishes the free pistol from the other types is the trigger. The lightweight trigger can be frightening to the shooter who is accustomed to a standard-weight trigger, but one quickly becomes used to it and at times it can appear to be just as heavy as a standard 2 pound trigger! This is because although the shooter thinks he is squeezing the trigger the reaction has been blocked before it reached his finger. It will happen when under stress.

There are several schools of thought about the best method of firing the free trigger. Three of these are:

(1) Direct contact with the trigger immediately the pistol is raised;

(2) Contact between trigger finger and trigger only when the sights are perfectly aligned;

(3) Intermittent touching of the trigger during aiming.

In method 3 the aim is taken with the forefinger flexed and with the pad that touches the trigger constantly fluttering backwards and forwards depending upon whether the aim is approaching a good one or not. If the aim is good then the finger closes up and if the aim remains stationary then the final pressure is applied. If the aim is not good enough then the finger is relaxed again. In this way the shooter can be ready to fire the pistol as soon as the aim has steadied. The disadvantages of this method are two-fold. Firstly the whole muscular effort is being devoted to holding the pistol still but this is being upset by the finger-tip being kept in constant motion. This movement of the finger-tip is not confined to that part of the finger but involves other muscles in the hand, some of which will be moving in contrary directions. These movements must have some effect on the ability to hold the aim. Secondly, this method can result in the trigger being released at the wrong moment. If the shooter has relaxed his finger and is approaching a good aim he may misjudge the position of his finger and the release may be too early or too late.

Method 2 is adopted by many shooters who use a very light trigger. If the trigger is very light, then there will be very little time lag between 'thinking' the shot off and actually firing the shot. It is during this very vital period that the pistol must be held quite still and the shorter this time the less chance there will be of the pistol going off the aim. This type of shooting is often called 'touch shooting' and can produce some very high scores if the shooter is in top form and his reaction time is quick. By reaction time is meant the time between recognizing the true aim and the implementing of the action required to fire the pistol. If the shooter is in top form the reaction time could be as fast as one-hundredth of a second, but if not it might be as slow as one-fifth of a second. Such a variation will mean that when the shooter is not in form then the pistol will have moved slightly off aim before the shot has been fired and a number of shots will be outside the normal group. This method of trigger control is conducive to accidental discharges for the slightest touch on the trigger will fire the gun. An unintentional quick movement when raising the gun with a very light trigger may accidentally fire it. In cold weather the finger-tip will not be as sensitive to touch and the shooter may not feel the trigger until after the shot has been fired! Under the amended rules for free pistol an accidental discharge counts as a shot to score if it hits anywhere on the target. If it misses the target, the firer may fire another

THE FREE PISTOL

round but with a 2 point penalty. A light trigger will be more prone to accidental discharge and under this rule the shooter will be penalized. This type of touch shooting is very vulnerable to nervous pressure.

It is therefore a logical conclusion that the first method should be the best. The trigger should be of sufficient weight to allow the finger to rest against it and confidently feel the trigger knowing that it will not fire accidentally at the slightest touch. The trigger finger should be placed gently but firmly on the trigger and as the concentration on the aim is maintained the pressure is steadily increased until the shot breaks. If the aim is not good then the finger can be relaxed and removed from the trigger and the gun then brought down.

The danger which all free-pistol shooters have to guard against is trigger shyness. This is the condition when the firer is afraid to release the trigger in case it goes off at the wrong moment. This can and must be overcome by positive action. The shooter must have confidence in his own ability and adopt a steadily increasing pressure on the trigger so that the shot will break when the aim is correct. That is to say: *the shot is fired when the aim is correct,* rather than: when the aim is correct the shot is fired. It is considered that the first method of shooting is the one that will give the necessary control to achieve this object. If the shooter progresses from standard pistol to free pistol then this method of trigger control is the same, except for the difference in trigger weight. He will not have to learn a completely different trigger technique but only adapt the one he has already learned.

When commencing the free-pistol match, the shooter will have a sighting or practice card exposed. He is permitted to fire a maximum of fifteen sighting shots. These may be fired at any time before the match cards are raised or during the interval between each ten-shot series and in emergencies as covered by the rules. The sighting shots are of vital importance. As the shooter will already know his normal zero setting of his sights, the sighting shots should be used to study the conditions of the range, light and wind and to bring the shooter to the proper state of mental tension and body relaxation before the record shoot. The sighting shots should be fired as far as possible as match shots so that the shooter is reinforcing his mental approach to the occasion. He should maintain a chart of his shots, both for calling the shot before he has spotted it and to record the strike of the shot on the target. He will then see where his group is falling at that particular time and make any adjustment necessary. This should take five to eight shots. After any sight adjustment he should fire another three shots to confirm that he has made the correct adjustment. This will leave him with four to seven practice shots in reserve should it be necessary to take further sighting shots during the match.

If the light is good, the shooter will be able to distinguish a smaller amount of light between the tip of the foresight and the aiming mark and therefore hold his aim closer to the black. This will put the group high and the backsight will have to be lowered a couple of clicks or so. If the light is dull then the opposite will apply and the sights will have to be raised. Most free-pistol sights are held against a spring and to raise the sight the screw is unscrewed or loosened to raise the sight and screwed down or tightened to lower it.

Sighting shots will also enable the shooter to judge any deflection caused by wind. This will not greatly affect the shot at 50 metres unless it is more than a gentle breeze. As a rough guide each click on the sights will move the group about the width of a shot hole at 50 metres. Wind adjustment should be made for the average wind as it is impossible to make continual adjustments for each shot. If the shooter did try to change for each shot he would soon be lost in a maze of wind changes and would be unable to regain his normal zero without reference to his records. Most good ranges are equipped with wind indicators between the firing point and the target, giving direction and strength. So long as the firer keeps a general eye on strength and direction he should not get himself into trouble. A diagonal wind will only require half the alteration of the same strength of wind directly across the range. A fore and aft wind is unlikely to affect the bullet in flight but will be more unpleasant to the

THE FREE PISTOL

shooter. The time allowed for the shoot is long enough for the shooter to be able to wait for the right conditions unless there is any material change in the average conditions.

To achieve the best performance with the free pistol the shooter must learn to fire the shot during the optimum performance period. This depends on four factors—breathing, trigger control, ability to hold, and concentration.

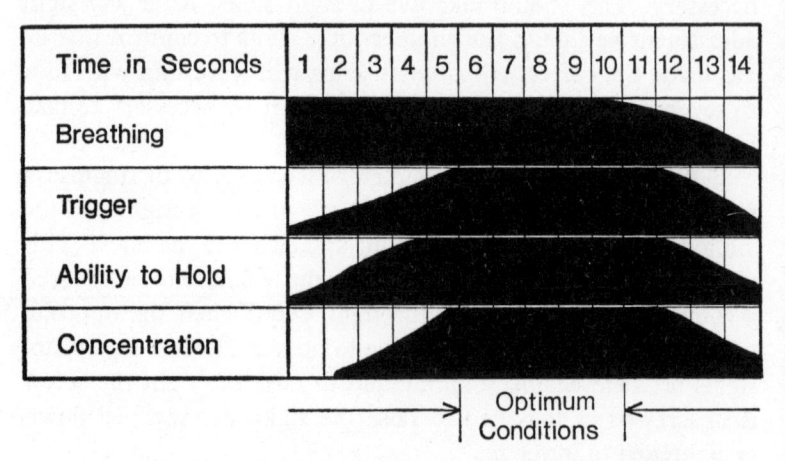

Time in Seconds	1	2	3	4	5	6	7	8	9	10	11	12	13	14
Breathing														
Trigger														
Ability to Hold														
Concentration														

Optimum Conditions

17. *Diagram showing optimum shooting conditions*

The breathing has to be restrained and the longer the time this is done the more the body will feel the lack of oxygenated blood. The pulse will increase and the mind will be distracted as the bodily discomfort intrudes on the concentration. So as far as this factor is concerned the sooner the shot is fired the better.

Trigger control is also time-governed. If the trigger is released too quickly there is the danger that the shot will be snatched. If the release is delayed too long then the shooter will try and rush the shot to coincide with an apparently good aim. At the extremities of the trigger control time there is the danger of a bad shot. The time which is considered best for trigger release is between six and ten seconds after bringing the pistol on aim.

The ability to hold depends upon the efficiency of the muscles which hold the weight of the pistol and the arm in the aiming position. Muscles become fatigued when under stress, as when trying to hold the pistol as close to the proper aiming mark as possible. A certain time is needed to allow the pistol to be brought on aim and the gun should not be fired before that time. The gun must not be held up too long or the muscles will be unable to hold it still. The time period here is estimated from five to eleven seconds after raising the pistol.

The last factor is concentration. The shooter cannot immediately concentrate on the aim as soon as the pistol is brought up, for he also has to think about bringing the pistol into the right position, placing his finger on the trigger and so on. The intense concentration on the aim will be built up after a few seconds but cannot be continued for long as the mental effort is severe. Concentration is at its best for a period from six to ten seconds after lifting up the pistol.

If all these factors are combined it will be seen from the diagram that the optimum conditions for firing the shot will obtain from six to ten seconds after bringing the pistol into the aiming position. This period of about five seconds is quite sufficient to fire the shot and should be considered whenever slow-fire shooting is concerned. It is not confined to free-pistol shooting.

To ensure that the pistol shooter does fire his shots during this period he must follow a methodical training programme. The programme should be such that the shooter builds up his firing techniques at the beginning of the shooting season. The first stage will be to build up the muscles which control the ability to hold. This can be done by lifting up the pistol to the aiming position and holding it there for periods of up to fifteen seconds. It is not necessary to use a pistol provided something of about the same weight is used. The number of times the pistol is lifted to and held in the aiming position should be gradually increased until the shooter can comfortably hold the pistol still over the full course of fire.

The next stage is to repeat this while at the same time exercising control over the trigger, but without paying attention to a precise aim. This will enable the reflexes to function so that the trigger is squeezed to break in six to ten seconds. A timer can be used, set at ten seconds and if the trigger has not been released at this time the pistol is lowered. After a spell at ten seconds, the time will be reduced to eight seconds. Having acquired the rhythm of holding the pistol up and squeezing the trigger, this exercise should then be combined with aiming and dry firing. The shooter can then proceed to actual firing and if he has established the rhythm as a conditioned reflex the shot will be fired at the optimum time.

It should be remembered that the follow through should be practised when dry firing as this is an essential part of the rhythm of firing.

Conditioned reflexes have been mentioned. When they are functioning the shooter will find that some of his shots have apparently been fired without conscious effort. The visual image has been accepted by the brain as correct without this having been a conscious act. The subsequent muscular action to finally release the trigger has also been unconscious. The reaction time of the brain in assessing the true picture and activating the next process as a reflex is virtually simultaneous. As the brain has recognized the correct image, the reflex shot is seldom far from the centre.

The shooter should plan his whole shoot before he starts but take into consideration any possible circumstance that may cause his original plan to be altered. He should assess all likely outside influences so that he will not be worried by these. The shooter should be able to plan when he wants to fire the shot and he will not fire a shot until he is ready to fire. For example, he should judge the weather and if he has previous knowledge of the local weather conditions he may know that the weather may change for the worse towards the end of the allotted time. In such circumstances, he would plan to fire quickly, rather losing a few points on account of firing quickly than losing more points because of the weather conditions. Perhaps the range conditions are such that instead of targets being changed from the butts at the firer's request, all shooting has to stop at fixed intervals to allow the target changers to change the targets in the open. The shooter will then have to plan to fire ten shots in a fixed time.

24. Parabolic mirror foresight. (*S. A. Hämmerli*)

25. Front of rearsight. (*S. A. Hämmerli*)

26. Target as viewed through normal sights. (*S. A. Hämmerli*)

27. Target as viewed with mirror sights. (*S. A. Hämmerli*)

28. The Asaka Range in Tokyo as used in the 1964 Olympic Games showing top screens or baffles and side screens. (*Shooting Sport*)

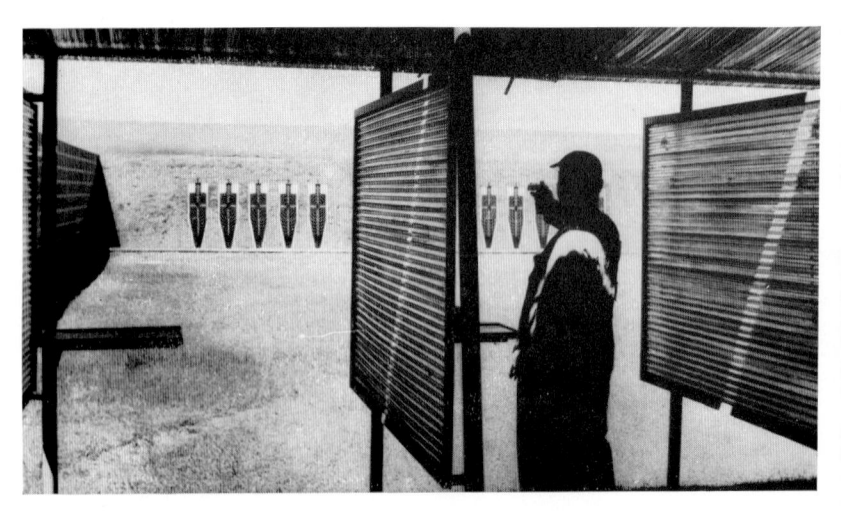

29. 25 metre Rapid Fire Range in Cairo as used in the 1962 World Championships. (*Shooting Sport*)

30. Hämmerli Rapid Fire Model 210. (*S. A. Hämmerli*)

31. Rapid Fire Grip. (Hämmerli ·22 short Olympia.) Good support for palm and fingers. Trigger finger falling naturally square on the trigger. (*Courtesy of A. J. Clark*)

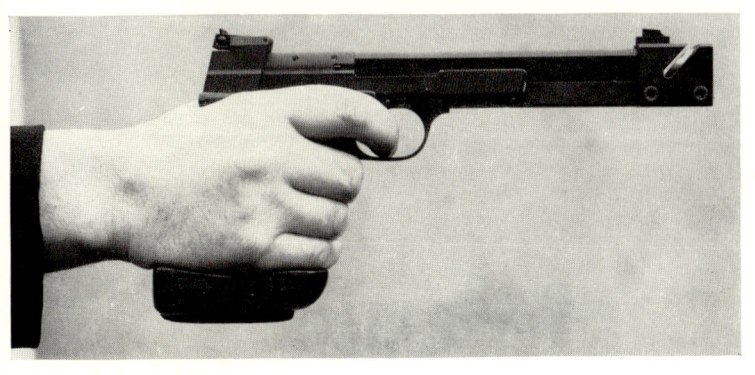

32. Opposite view of 31. (*Courtesy of A. J. Clark*)

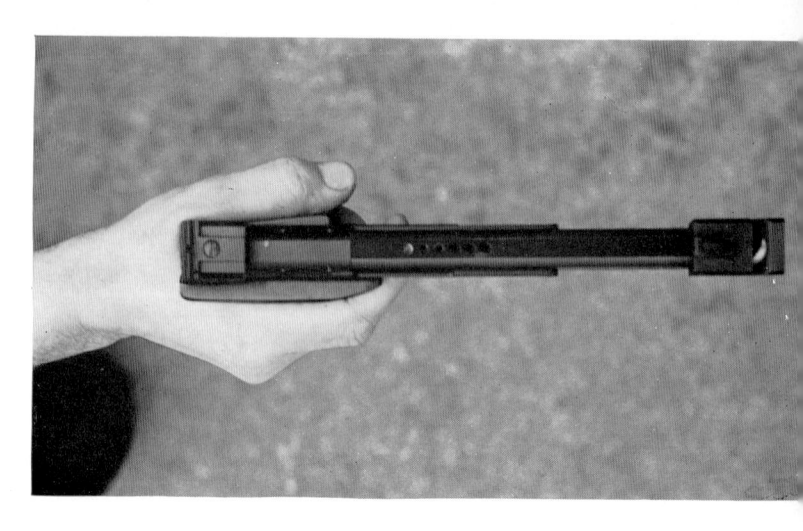

33. Rapid Fire Grip (top view). This shows the angle the wrist is turned the vertical plane to bring the sights in line. (*Courtesy of A. J. Clark*)

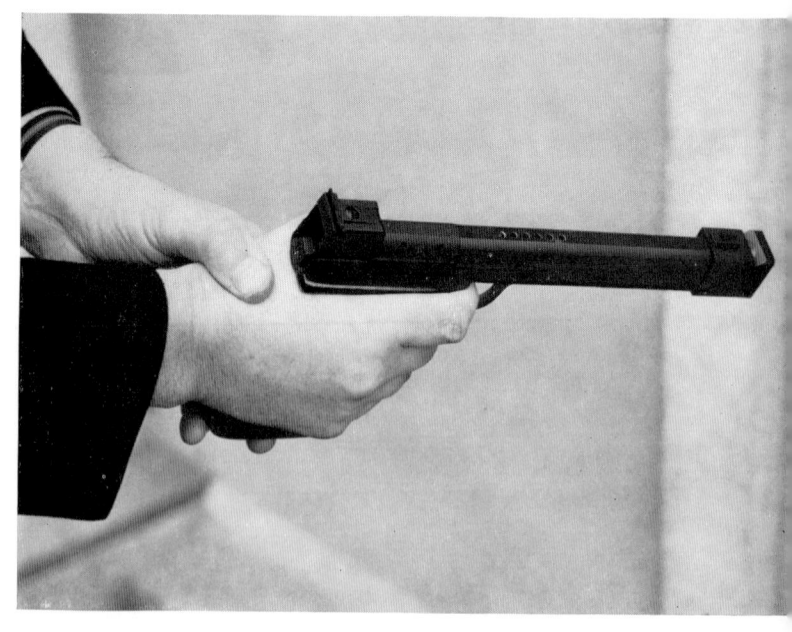

34. Tightening the grip by pulling back the skin so that slide will not fo the proud flesh. Note that this is done with the grip in the firing positio i.e. finger on trigger. (*Courtesy of A. J. Clark*)

THE FREE PISTOL

Different shooters fire at different rates and a new shooter will often raise the question as to which rate is the best. This is something the shooter will have to find out for himself but certain guide lines can be laid down. If the shooter fires all his sighting shots and his match shots he will have fired seventy-five shots in a permitted time of two and a half hours or an average of one shot every two minutes. Assuming that the shot breaks first time then the shooter has one minute fifty seconds between each shot. If the shooter is shooting well he may have fired five shots in less than five minutes and thinks to himself, 'I should have taken ten minutes.' The shooter should fire the next shot when he feels that he is ready to do so; he should not make a fetish of the clock. He should, however, consider the long time that the shoot is occupying and therefore that he has time to rest between shots or series of shots.

The shooter must take sufficient rest between each shot to allow the mind and body to shoot the following shot at maximum efficiency. Recovery time is quite quick but will tend to lengthen as the shoot progresses. If the shooter finds himself having to make several attempts to fire the shot, then he is using up physical and mental energy. During his training he should strive to co-ordinate the eye and muscle so that the shot is fired at the first attempt. If this is achieved then the firer can give himself plenty of time and if necessary long intervals of rest knowing that when he does start again he will be able to keep to any schedule that he sets himself.

The interval between the shots must be a time of positive relaxation. The shooter can put the gun down between each shot or he may prefer to remain in the shooting position and fire a number of shots before putting the gun down. Whichever way he prefers he should still relax between shots. If he makes a complete break between shots then he will put the gun down, check the shot and then sit down and relax the mind and body until it is time to fire the next shot. He should then resume the proper firing position and bring his mind to bear on firing the next shot with the proper technique. He will have taken into account the position of the previous shot but will approach each

18. *Record card*

Lay-out: Otto Horber

shot separately from the last. If the shooter remains in the firing position for a few shots, he should still relax momentarily between shots by relaxing his grip for a moment and looking away from the target at a restful colour, and so divorce himself from the previous shot.

The shooter should keep a record of his shoot, shot by shot, so that he can study it after the shoot to see if there is any pattern which needs analysis. The record should be compiled between shots first by putting the position of the called shot before comparing it with the position of the shot on the target.

Score cards form a valuable record for study as the shooter will give all the details of the shoot including the light, weather, wind etc. He will find under which conditions and at what time of day he shoots best and where his weaknesses are. Record books can be bought commercially or made up by the shooter to his own requirements. A page of a score book is reproduced opposite and the most important column is the one headed 'calling'. By using this column with honest intent the shooter will have the best guide of the correctness of his technique. If the shot strikes the target close to the position that he thought it should, then he will be shooting correctly. The actual strike of the shot should be marked boldly on the diagram with a dot and a number beside it to indicate the order of firing. As it is desirable to treat each shot separately and not be distracted by knowing the running total of the score, the last column showing the value of the score should not be completed until the end of the shoot. If the shooter is shooting well and is likely to produce a high score he may worry himself out of a high score by knowing the actual figures. Similarly if he is finding it hard going, then it can only make matters worse if he knows that his previous shots have not produced a very high total. It is a very natural thing to do to consider and conjecture what the final score might be but if the shooter can disregard this then he will be able to concentrate on each shot to the full and produce a better score.

In a big match there will be many shooters of the same technical ability but it will be the shooter who has the determination to apply his ability to the full who will produce the highest score.

11

Rapid-Fire Shooting

This chapter will deal with ·22 rapid-fire shooting at both stationary and turning targets. The shooting at stationary targets falls under two headings, timed fire and rapid fire. The turning target shooting is the rapid-fire silhouette course shot under the rules of the Union International de Tir.

The targets for timed and rapid fire are similar to the standard deliberate shooting targets, but the scoring rings are twice the diameter. The shoot is normally ten shots on each target fired in two series or 'strings' of five shots. In timed fire five shots are fired in twenty seconds and in rapid fire it is five shots in ten seconds. This course must be shot with a semi-automatic weapon or a revolver.

The essence of shooting any timed or rapid fire course is good rhythm and this will only be acquired with practice. The time must be used to the full and there is very little difference in technique between the timed and rapid course.

The normal specification when firing these two courses is that the match will be of thirty shots. The first ten will be deliberate slow fire and this will be followed by ten shots timed and then ten shots rapid. Under some rules it is obligatory to use the same pistol for the whole match. The shooter will know the zero for his gun after firing the deliberate course and will have found from experience whether he has any need to make any sight adjustment for the timed match.

The shooter will therefore arrive at the firing point with a correctly sighted pistol. This is important as whilst there will

RAPID-FIRE SHOOTING

normally be a practice series before the match card there will be only one opportunity for adjustment of sights if the zero is found to be off centre. In the preparatory period before going to the firing point the shooter will check his equipment and mentally go through the course of fire counting out the rhythm in his mind. He will look at the conditions and reconstruct the good scores that he has made under such conditions. He will then approach the firing point in the right frame of mind to produce a good score.

It is, of course, necessary in this type of shooting as in others to know the fundamental principles. They are the same for all pistol shooting. First, the ability to hold the pistol within a minimum arc of movement, secondly to achieve proper sight alignment, and third to apply constant progressive trigger pressure until the shot breaks.

To apply these principles to timed and rapid fire, the shooter must have full knowledge of the course of fire. The rules and fire commands for these courses of fire will vary from place to place and the shooter must know the rules for the particular competition in which he will be participating. Under some rules, such as N.S.R.A., he will be permitted to be on aim before the actual command to fire is given whilst other rules state that the pistol must be at an angle of 45 degrees or resting on the bench until the order 'fire' is given. Either a verbal command will be given or firing will commence on the appearance of the targets after the shooters having been given a cautionary command. The aim will be at the aiming mark or at the point where the aiming mark will appear when the targets are faced. The aim must be a natural one and must be tested before shooting commences during the preparation period allowed at the firing point. This is best done by raising the arm to the firing position with the eyes shut. On opening the eyes, the shooter will observe whether the aim is to the right or to the left and will adjust his stance until the arm comes up in line with the aiming mark. The stance should be open with the weight evenly placed on both feet. It should be remembered that the arm will have to be kept in the aiming position throughout the shoot and if the body is comfortably balanced there is little chance that the pistol will be deflected from the line of natural aim during the shoot.

The grip on the pistol must be firm as it has to withstand the shock of five shots without relaxation between them. Great care must be taken when taking the grip to see that the hand is pushed tightly into the grip whilst holding the gun barrel with the free hand. Then the small folds of flesh that are exposed on the edges should be pushed down with the free hand to ensure complete contact between the hand and the grip. Once the grip is taken it should not be altered until the string is fired. As this grip will be tiring it should not be adopted until just before firing.

The firer has now taken the correct grip and stance, and assuming he has trained himself to hold the gun still he will have applied the first two principles. The third principle of trigger pressing is vital to a good rapid-fire shoot. The trigger must be pressed with a constant pressure in a line straight back through the pistol. This will help the pistol to remain on alignment with the target. Immediately the shot is fired the pressure on the trigger must be released allowing it to return to its initial position, the slack is then taken up and the progressive pressure reapplied until the next shot is fired and the cycle again repeated.

The first shot is important. Whether the pistol is permitted to be on aim or not, a precautionary word of command is given followed very shortly by the executive word of command or by the appearance of the targets. The progressive pressure can be started after the warning order is given so that the first shot will be fired within a second of the start whether in timed or rapid fire. The remaining shots will be fired in a regular rhythm that the firer has learned during training, so that he will finish the shoot with about 0·5 seconds left. One can tell the better shooters by listening to the rhythm and timing of their shooting.

The shooter in the timed fire has twenty seconds to fire five shots and this will mean that he will have to take a fresh breath half-way through the string as he will not be able to hold his breath comfortably for the whole time. He will be ready to shoot just before the word of command is given and should therefore have restrained his breath just after the cautionary word of command has been given. He should then take a quick breath after his third shot. His first shot will have been fired within the first second of starting, so his third shot will be fired at about eleven seconds after starting which will be about thirteen seconds after he restrained his breathing. This is about the limit to which the breathing should be restrained. The rapid-fire course will be fired without having to take a breath in the middle.

The shooter has now observed the three fundamentals but will have to consider slight changes in technique. During his preparation on the firing point the shooter will have adopted the proper stance that will give him a central group. During the firing of the string he has no chance of seeing the target and then changing his focus to the sights and taking a deliberate aim. He will as usual have to concentrate on the foresight throughout the string and see that it remains square in the backsight notch. If the shooter has ensured that he is sighted in properly then the shots will form a central group. Even if the aim is slightly off centre but the sights are in their proper relation then the errors will only be parallel and the score will not suffer greatly.

When the shot is fired the shooter will have a mental picture of the relation of the sights to each other. Even though the time is short he will be attempting to maintain this proper relation by conditioned reflexes. The gun will move out of proper alignment due to recoil, but if it is held firmly then it will fall back to the sights alignment controlled by the stance. To reduce the effect of recoil and to ensure a more rapid recovery to the original position, the elbow must be locked and the arm pushed forward a little more than in deliberate shooting. The arm will then recover to the correct position for the next shot and whilst the positive pressure is being taken the very slight adjustments in the aim are being made. This can be done if the shooter is concentrating hard on the foresight. It is tempting to glance at the target to see if the gun is properly aligned but if the shooter is confident that he has the proper stance and is gripping the gun correctly then the pistol must continue to point in the same direction.

RAPID-FIRE SHOOTING

The double size of the scoring rings takes account of the fact that the group will be larger than that when shooting slow fire. With practice high scores can be achieved. The top shooters should not be satisfied with a score of under 195 for ten shots timed and ten shots rapid. It is interesting to observe that some shooters will fire a better group in rapid fire than in slow fire. This will certainly be due to the fact that in rapid fire the shooter will consistently take the progressive trigger pressure. In deliberate shooting he will dwell too long on the aim to try and get the perfect shot and so will make faults in his technique.

Fault analysis and correction is not to be overlooked. Even though the shooting is a consecutive sequence of five shots, the mental impression after the shoot will be of five distinct shots and so the shooter should have the ability to state the relative aim of each shot. He might say that 1, 3 and 5 were central, for No. 2 the foresight was a bit low and that for No. 4 the foresight blade was a little to the right. If the errors were not excessive the shots could still all be in the 10 ring, with one high and the other just hanging on at 4 o'clock. This would give the shooter warning that he must make a more rapid adjustment of his foresight within the backsight as he is releasing the shot.

If the group itself was off centre then there are two things that could be wrong. Either the stance is incorrect or the pistol is off zero. If this has happened in the practice session, then the shooter has to make up his mind which is wrong. If he says that his stance might have been wrong and the following string to score is also off centre then he has penalized himself. He must be confident that his stance is correct. One must therefore presuppose that the group is off centre due to an incorrect zero. This must be corrected and corrected boldly. The shooter should know, for the gun he is using, exactly what difference alteration of the sight will make at the distance he is shooting. There is no opportunity for a second chance. It is therefore vital that the practice string is shot exactly as for the match and not just as a warming-up exercise.

If the group is larger than would be expected then the shooter is either not paying attention to details or his gun is not in

RAPID-FIRE SHOOTING

first-class condition. No shooter should try and shoot for a high score unless he is quite satisfied with the condition of his gun and he has only himself to blame in this respect. To tighten up his group he must go over each point in the technique to see that he has mastered all the detail and that he fires with the determination to succeed. There is very little time to feel nervous nor to dwell on mistakes except to learn from them.

If the group is a good central one then the shooter should make a careful analysis of his method. He will then be able to repeat the performance on the next occasion. A good score is no excuse for complacency.

Probably the hardest lesson to learn is the rhythm of firing. The first shot will break at the latest one second after the firing command has been given and the last shot at nineteen seconds in the timed fire and 9·5 seconds in the rapid fire. In the timed fire the shooter has an interval of 4·5 seconds between each shot and in rapid fire 2·1 seconds. These timings can be practised by dry shooting using a metronome set for the intervals. Practice should be continued until the shooter has the interval times fixed in his mind so that he will fire by conditioned reflex once the word of command is given. He will then be able to concentrate on maintaining the aim. Such practice will give the shooter the confidence to shoot a good score each time.

The other major rapid-fire course for ·22 weapons is the match at silhouette targets under international rules. The target is a black silhouette target as illustrated, 1·6 metres in length and ·45 metres in width at the widest part. The centre scoring zone (ten points) is 10 centimetres wide and 15 centimetres high at its apogee, each scoring zone increases by 5 centimetres either side and 7·5 centimetres top and bottom. The targets will be in groups of five for each shooter, the centre of one target being 75 centimetres from the centre of the adjacent target. They will be so mounted that they each turn through an angle of 90 degrees at the same time and that the turning time will not exceed 0·1 seconds in either direction. The match is of sixty shots, shot in two courses of thirty shots. Each course is shot in six series of five shots and in each course two five-shot series are shot at

RAPID-FIRE SHOOTING

each of the following time intervals of exposure: eight, six and four seconds. The shooter is allowed one five-shot practice series at the beginning of each course, the timing being at his discretion. If there are in use more than one set of apparatus then the shooters will fire each thirty-shot course at a different set to negate any advantage due to position. In post-war competitions and until 1956 the order of merit was decided by total number of hits and then total score so that a shooter with a greater number of hits could be higher in the order of placing than a competitor with a greater score but a lesser number of hits. This meant that there was greater merit in hitting the target anywhere than in trying for a high score. This was a relic of the pre-war days when there were no scoring rings on the targets and only hits counted. The latest amendment to the rules means that the competitor with the greater score would win irrespective of the number of hits. This has undoubtedly improved the standard of shooting as all competitors must try for a high score and to achieve this all shots must be on the target.

The method of conducting the shoot is for the range official to call a squad of shooters to the firing point and after seeing that their pistols have been passed by weapons control and are in accordance with the rules, allow them the necessary time to prepare their equipment and themselves for the match. When the range official considers that the shooter is ready he will inquire whether this is so. The shooters will fire one at a time and when the first shooter is ready he will call 'Ready'. Up to this time the targets will be edgeways on to the shooter but despite this he has been able to line himself up. On hearing the word 'Ready' the range officer will make a signal and after a short delay of two to four seconds the targets will turn through 90 degrees and face the shooter. The shooter must maintain his arm at an angle of not less than 45 degrees to the horizontal until the targets commence to turn to face the shooter.

When the targets are exposed the firer will raise his arm and fire one shot at each of the five targets within the given time. The targets will turn away at the end of the time and will then be faced again so that they may be scored by another official.

RAPID-FIRE SHOOTING

The strike of the shots will either be indicated at the targets by means of white or red discs or the shooter may spot them with a telescope. After the targets have been scored and the range is clear, the shooter will reload with five rounds and prepare himself for the next series.

Having briefly described the match, it is now necessary to examine the problems that face the shooter and explain how they may be solved. The shooter has to raise his pistol in the shortest possible time commensurate with the taking of a steady aim at the first target. He then has to release the shot quickly but smoothly and accurately and then move the pistol across the remaining four targets firing one shot at each in the limited time that he has available to do all this.

The first shot of a five-shot series is the vital one as the other four depend on the smooth let off and accurate placing of the first. The shooter must therefore develop a very fast reaction to the movement of the target. The shooter must learn to lift his arm as soon as the targets begin to move without having to make a conscious effort. In other words this movement must become a conditioned reflex. As soon as the targets turn the arm will be raised fairly quickly until the line is about the 7 ring and then the movement will be slowed down until the pistol comes to rest in the centre of the target. It has been found that the most suitable aim is at the point of impact of the bullet, i.e. the target centre. A number of prominent rapid-fire shooters prefer to aim at about the figure 9 underneath the centre of the target as they think that this gives a much more definite point to aim at. Their pistol sights are adjusted to bring the centre of the group into the 10 ring. The object of this procedure is to get the correct aim at once. If the arm is brought up too slowly time is wasted; if too fast the arm will swing above the point of aim and will have to be brought down which again wastes time. As much time as possible has to be spent aiming at the correct point. To spot the first movement of the target the shooter will be looking at the target out of the corner of his eye but as soon as his arm starts coming up he must concentrate on his sights and keep looking at them as he raises his arm making adjustments to keep the relative positions of the foresight and backsight correct. To add a further burden to the shooter, he will also have taken the slack of the trigger when he called 'Ready' and as the arm is brought up he will be progressively taking the trigger pressure.

The correct aim is dependent on the correct stance and this is very much a matter for the individual in the final detail. The majority of shooters adopt the so called 'duelling' stance in which a line across the toes points in the direction of the targets. Others adapt this position to suit themselves by moving the front foot to the right or left. The feet are open to about the width of the shoulders to obtain a good balance for the body and the weight of the body should be taken equally on both feet. To make sure that the position is correct the shooter will make trial lifts of his arm in the same rhythm as he will fire. The pistol must come up in the proper vertical line through the centre of the first target. If it does not then the feet must be moved until the upward line is correct and this must be confirmed at least three times.

As has already been mentioned the first reaction must be fast. This is helped by adopting a slightly forward leaning position of the body when the arm is in the ready position. The pistol will be held firmly with the arm extended. When the targets turn the arm will be lifted and the back straightened and at the finish the body may be leaning back slightly. By using both arm and back the gun will be positioned on aim a little quicker.

As there are five targets to hit, it is necessary to consider which is the correct one to fire at first, and on which the stance should be aligned. With the modern pistol, the recoil can be reduced to a minimum and muzzle brakes adjusted to help carry the pistol from one target to another. The arm will move more naturally when moving from the shoulder towards the centre rather than away from the centre as the farther it moves from the centre the more resistance will be felt from the shoulder socket. Strain on the muscles and sinews must be avoided and therefore it is best to move the arm in the inward direction. The shooter will take up his position opposite the centre target, but take his stance to line up with the last target to be hit. The trial aim will be taken at the first target by swivelling the body through the hips and looking at the first target. The feet must not be moved and as the shooter moves his aim from one target to another his body will turn as his head moves to keep the proper sight alignment. With the right-handed shooter this means that he will take his stance so that the natural aim will be on the left-hand target but he will make his practice aims at the right-hand target. When he starts to fire the natural movement of his body and arm combined with the adjusted recoil of the pistol will help to bring the pistol across the targets in a smooth sequence.

The trigger may be set to any weight but the majority of shooters find that about 6 ounces is most suitable. It must be light enough for a smooth and fast release but not so light that the shots break too early. If it is too heavy then the shots will take too long to release. The actual weight which is best for each shooter will be found after experiment. The trigger weight must not vary and must be very positive in its action. The actual movement of the trigger must be kept to a minimum to give the shooter greater control over it. The pressure on the trigger has to be released after each shot and the smaller the amount of movement the shooter's trigger finger has to make to achieve this the more time he will have for that movement. If the trigger is too light then there is the danger of accidental discharges both by the shooter himself and also from the mechanism of the gun due to the sear being unable to hold in position in the hammer bent. A type of trigger known as a 'roll over' trigger has been introduced into some rapid-fire pistols. There is no clean-cut release with these but an apparent indeterminate release which is very difficult to judge.

The importance of the trigger mechanism means that the shooter must be meticulous in the care of his weapon. He must know how the pistol functions but should not attempt any adjustments to the mechanism unless he is sufficiently competent to do so. The smallest piece of fouling or grit can upset the fine adjustment of the pistol and this could cause a malfunction of the weapon in the middle of a shoot. The mechanism must be kept clean and correctly lubricated. The shooter must learn which is the correct lubricant for his weapon and how lubrication differs under differing climatic conditions. If the air is dusty then the minimum of lubrication should be used to enable the gun to function. If the gun will not function without a fair amount of lubrication then in such conditions it must be protected except for the moments it is required for shooting, and it should also be cleaned between shoots.

The commonest form of dirt in the mechanism is from the cartridge lubricant. It is wise to clean the cartridges before firing and also to see that the bullets are of uniform size. Cartridges should only be cleaned of *excess* lubricant and this is best done by wiping them either with the fingers or very gently with a dry cloth. Some shooters go to the trouble of sizing each cartridge to the chamber of their pistol so that in the match the cartridges will slide easily into the chamber and there will be no possibility of a malfunction due to a faulty size of cartridge. Other shooters douse the loaded magazine with thin oil to ensure that the cartridges feed easily into the chamber.

Stance and trigger let-off have been considered. The aim in conjunction with these will determine where the shot will hit the target. The target is black and the normal sights are also black and therefore the sights will not be readily distinguishable against the target when the sights are well illuminated, unless they are heavily but evenly coated with acetylene black when they will appear blacker than the target. When the targets have the greater illumination the sights will appear silhouetted against the target and their relative positions easily determined. If the sights are well illuminated their relative positions will not be so apparent and time will be lost in correcting them. The shooter will have to concentrate more on this aspect to the detriment of others and the score will suffer. To overcome this problem the sights can be coloured so they are readily distinguishable against the target. The front sight can be painted white or yellow and the backsight red. The colours should be matt so that direct light is not reflected off them to confuse the aim. In an emergency or if a permanent change is not required, chalk can be used. The sights may either be painted or replaced by plastic sights made of material of the required colour.

The firer must ensure that when he raises his arm the front sight is centred in the backsight. To start with he will be looking at the target out of the corner of his eye but as soon as the targets commence to turn he will look along his arm to pick up the sights and see that they are properly aligned. When the first shot is fired the pistol will jump a little from the recoil and at the same time the body will be turning to bring the arm across in the direction of the next target. The trigger finger will have relaxed its pressure on the trigger so that the mechanism of the gun can function to reload and recock. If the shooter does not relax his finger on the trigger after he has fired, he will find that next time he presses it nothing happens. This does happen in the early stages when a shooter is learning rapid-fire shooting as he is so intent on the other techniques that he forgets the trigger.

As the arm brings the pistol from one target to the next the trigger finger will begin to take the progressive trigger pressure. As the sights reach about the 8 ring on the targets the movement will be checked, and will cease when the sights are lined up on the 10 ring. The final pressure will be applied and the shot fired whilst the sights are stationary. The same procedure will be applied to each target and to an imaginary one beyond the fifth one. This 'follow through' is to ensure that the rhythm is continued to make sure of a good shot at the last target. The shot at each target must be fired when the arm has become stationary. This may only be for a fraction of a second but if the shooter has maintained the correct sight relationship during the movement from one target to the next and is progressively pressing the trigger, then he will only need a very short time to release a good shot.

The very rhythm of firing rapid-fire silhouettes imparts the finesse to the fundamental principles involved. The shooter has eight, six and four seconds to fire five shots and each of these times will have its own rhythm. It has been stressed that the first shot must be fired as quickly as possible and the last shot should not be delayed until the targets have turned. Taking the eight-second series first, the first shot should be fired in about two seconds. The same uplift of the arm will be used for each series and this will take about 0·8 seconds. In the eight-second series the shooter then has 1·2 seconds to fire his shot, which is ample time to make sure it is a good 10. He then has 5·7 seconds to fire the remaining four shots, or in other words an interval of 1·4 seconds between each shot. If the first shot is delayed 0·3 seconds and is not fired until 2·3 seconds the shooter still has time to shoot in his rhythm of 1·4 seconds. He must get this timing fixed in his mind so that he knows that, providing he is shooting in this rhythm, he has plenty of time for each shot.

As the eight-second series gives the shooter the longest time, it should give him the highest score, and he must strive to achieve the best possible score in this series. The first shot must be a ten and the time the shooter allows himself for this shot ensures that it is a ten. If the gun comes up right in the first place, then he has the additional time to steady the aim. If it does not come up quite right then he still has time to make adjustments to be sure of a ten.

The six-second series is a little harder than the eight and so the shooter must make sure that his gun comes up on the right aim first time. He will have already fired one practice series and two series of eight seconds, so he will have these shoots to give him confidence. The first shot should break not later than 1·6 seconds after the start. This will give the shooter an interval of one second for each of the subsequent shots. In this string the gun will be gripped just a little bit tighter and the muscles will feel a little more tense. This series should give the shooter the chance of a high score, but there will be little time to make any alterations in aim once the shooting has commenced.

The four-second series is, of course, the hardest as there is no time to correct error. If the shooter does come up slightly off centre on the first shot, he does not have time to correct his aim and must fire when the gun reaches the correct height. It will be the fault of the firer if he is not on the right vertical

35. Rapid Fire Stance: (1) Waiting for target to turn. Note: Heels at shoulder width, arm extended with straight wrist, eye on target.

36. Opposite view of 35.

37. Rapid Fire Stance: (2) Target has turned. Note: Arm being raised, pistol being brought up with straight arm, eye on sights.

38. Opposite view of 37.

39. Rapid Fire Stance: (3) Shooting position. Note: To achieve final lift body has been straightened and is now slightly bent back. Left hand thrust into pocket.

40. Opposite view of 39.
(Plates 35–40, courtesy of A. J. Clark)

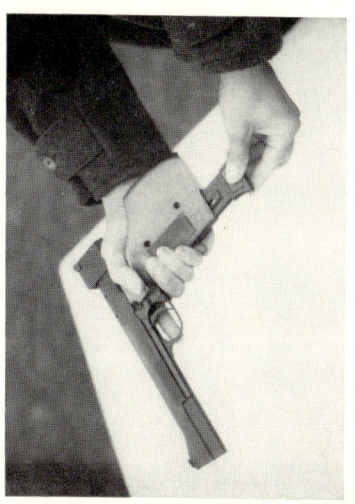

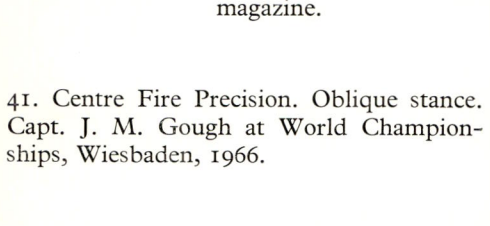

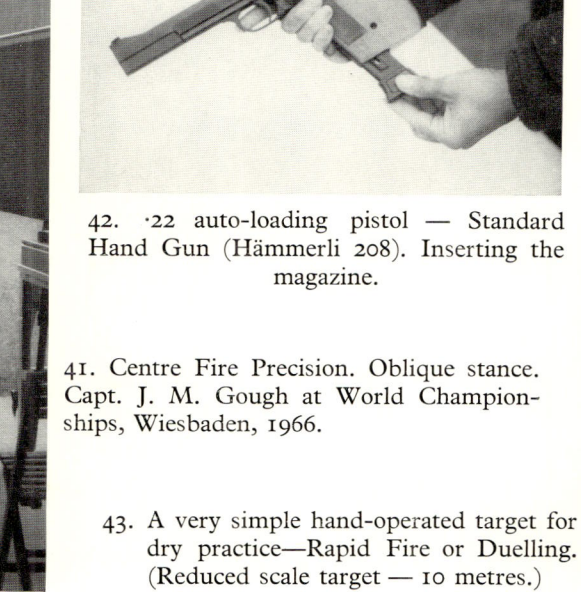

42. ·22 auto-loading pistol — Standard Hand Gun (Hämmerli 208). Inserting the magazine.

41. Centre Fire Precision. Oblique stance. Capt. J. M. Gough at World Championships, Wiesbaden, 1966.

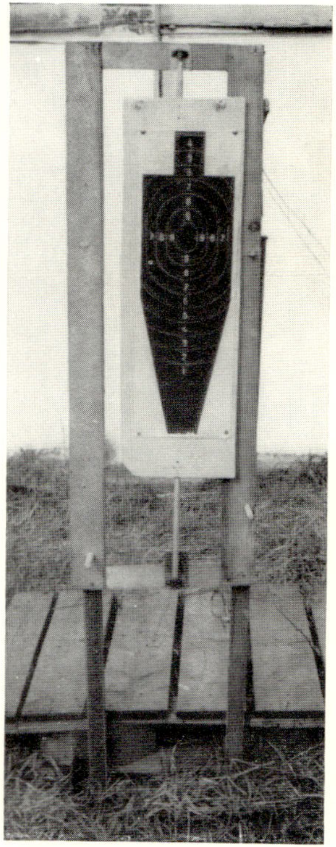

43. A very simple hand-operated target for dry practice—Rapid Fire or Duelling. (Reduced scale target — 10 metres.)

44. Centre Fire—the revolver grip.

45. Centre Fire—taking the grip. Barrel held with left hand whilst right hand is correctly positioned.

RAPID-FIRE SHOOTING

line as he must always check his stance before he calls 'Ready'. If his stance is correct the least he should score on his first shot is a nine. It is preferable to get this, rather than to try and correct for a ten. In doing so he will lose too much time, lose his rhythm for the remaining shots and finish with a poor score. The rhythm for the four-second series should be for the first shot to break at one second and the remainder at intervals of 0·7 seconds giving a total time for the shooter of 3·8 seconds.

The uplift should be the same for each series and so should the movement from target to target, which will be about 0·5 seconds. The difference therefore in each series is only the time that the shooter has to remain still at each target. In the eight-second series this will be 0·9 seconds, in the six-second one it will be 0·5 seconds and in the four-second series 0·2 seconds.

The acquisition of the rhythm can only come through constant practice and it is suggested that the following methods of training be adopted. First the action of raising the arm and firing the first shot within the time limit suggested should be practised. This will be done time after time as a single shot until the firer is sure to score a ten. The shot should be fired as if for each of the series, that is in 2, 1·6 and 1 second respectively. It helps considerably if the shooter has an assistant with a stop watch to time the break of the shot.

Having mastered these times, the shooter will go on to fire the remaining four shots, but without any time limit. This will be done on stationary targets. The object here is to develop the correct swing from target to target and to train the muscles to hold the arm at the proper height throughout the shoot. The shooter will try to achieve a ten on each target and only when he can do this consistently should he begin to fire within the time limits.

Practice without actually shooting can help to develop the proper rhythm. Miniature targets are available scaled down to as short a distance as 5 metres and these can be put up in a room at home and used at any convenient time. A metronome is a valuable training aid when set at the interval times. When dry practising the effort should be the same as if actually shooting

RAPID-FIRE SHOOTING

and any faults detected must be analysed at once and the remedy practised until they are eradicated. Repeating CO_2 operated 'Air' pistols have been developed that will simulate rapid-fire shooting and therefore actual firing can be practised away from the range and even in the home.

Every opportunity for practice should be taken and even at a big match the shooter waiting to fire will be seen having a dry run whilst the next shooter is firing his course.

There are three more factors that will help the shooter to gain a good score. The stocks of the pistol must be made to fit the shooter and must be fitted to the gun at the correct angle. This is the angle made between the hand and the gun when on aim. The detail for these grips will be the same as for other pistols except that the grip must not be more than 5 centimetres in width. It is quite possible within these limits to make the grip with a narrow band at the back of the hand. Breathing will be the same as for the other types of shooting. The shooter will restrain his breathing just after he has called ready and will begin to concentrate before the targets turn. There is one other point and that is the disengaged hand. This should not be left hanging free but should preferably be put into a pocket to help to support the body. A loose hand is useless.

There are some faults that can be seen from the pattern of the shots on the target. These faults can all be remedied by practice. There will be shots fired at the right height but displaced to the left or right. If the shooter is making an error the pattern will be consistent. The shots would form quite a small group if put together on one target. The lateral displaced group is because the firer is releasing the trigger too early or too late. If too early the shots will be on the right and if too late they will be on the left. The fault is that the shooter is firing whilst the pistol is moving; he has not trained himself to fire only when it is stationary. He is probably over-anxious and will not wait and thinks that he only has time to fire whilst the pistol is passing across the target. These patterns should only occur when the shooter is learning the techniques and should be eradicated when he has had sufficient practice.

RAPID-FIRE SHOOTING

Another pattern is that with the shots going away in a line from the centre at either 2 o'clock or 4 o'clock. The former will be due to the shooter not having taken a firm grip on the pistol so that the recoil throws the gun up from his grip. A firmer hold should cure this. When the shots go down, this will be due to faulty trigger release. The shooter is anxious to fire the shots as soon as the pistol comes on to the centre of the target and will snatch the trigger. To cure this the trigger must be progressively pressed as it moves from one target to the other and finally released only when the gun is still. The release must be smooth and straight back. The trigger finger must be quite free and the grip made so that the first pad comes naturally on to the trigger.

If the group is high or low then the simple answer is to alter the sights. The shooter must maintain the same lift of the arm and should not try to alter the group by trying to aim higher or lower. The eye must be concentrating on the sights and not on the target. The sight setting for this match should be constant and should be recorded by the shooter so that if he does shoot other competitions with the pistol having different sight settings he can quickly adjust his sights to the zero for the match.

The condition of the pistol is very important. If there is a malfunction then the shooter is likely to incur a penalty. In slow fire the shooter will have time to remedy a defect or change his pistol but the rapid-fire shooter has no time for this. A malfunction may be allowed and a reshoot permitted if the fault in the weapon or ammunition is outside the control of the shooter, i.e. the chamber contains a round with the clear imprint of the firing pin on the primer. In any case of a malfunction the shooter must immediately place his gun on the table and call the attention of the range official to the malfunction. He must not in any circumstances attempt to open or otherwise manipulate the gun, or a valid malfunction will not be allowed. However, a malfunction must have some effect on the equanimity of the shooter and it is better not to have one at all than be allowed a reshoot. Only two valid malfunctions are allowed in each half course. In the event of the gun breaking or failing to function at all, it may be replaced with another similar weapon but the shooter will not be allowed a further practice string. Shooters should study very carefully the rules governing the competition as contravention of them can incur severe penalties.

The shooter will be permitted to have normal shooting aids on the firing point. He should wear ear protectors which in addition to protecting his ears will assist in his concentration. Clothing must be loose as any restriction will hamper the movements of his arm; track suits are popular.

Rapid-fire shooting is an enjoyable form of pistol shooting, not only for the shooter but for the spectator. Shooting is not really a spectator sport as unless there is close-circuit television or similar visual aids, the spectator cannot see where the shots are striking. In this competition he can see something and as soon as the shooter has finished the markers will place discs in the shotholes to indicate the position of the strike.

A very good film of rapid-fire shooting was produced during the 1964 Olympic Games in Tokyo. This film shows many of the best rapid-fire shooters competing in the Olympics and illustrates their actions in normal, slow and ultra-slow motion. The firmness of grip, the smoothness of movement and the stillness of position when firing was common to all shooters. An interesting question is posed by one of the sequences where the shooter's pulse rate was superimposed over his time of firing. Where the pulse coincided with the release of the shot, the shooter scored his only shot off centre. Does this mean that shooters in this standard of competition have to take into account even their pulse rate when they are developing their own rhythm?

On 1st January 1968 a standard pistol event was introduced into the U.I.T. programme. The match, fired at 25 metres on the precision target, consists of 60 shots. 20 shots are fired in 4 series of 5 shots in 150 seconds, in 20 seconds and in 10 seconds. Only one series of 5 sighting shots is allowed. In this competition the arm must be kept at an angle of 45 degrees until the targets are exposed. The pistol must conform to the C.F. regulations, except that the trigger weight must not be less than 1 kilogram and only ·22 long rifle ammunition is permitted.

12

Centre Fire

It is not proposed to discuss in detail the merits of any particular centre-fire pistol but to point out that centre-fire target shooting has developed from military shooting. The standard issue for the British Army for a long time was the revolver of ·45 or similar calibre but this was superseded in the 1930's by calibres of ·32 to ·38. The modern military pistols are semi-automatic using 9 millimetre. The modern target shooter will use a ·38 special calibre revolver or semi-automatic chambered for the ·38 special revolver cartridge. There is apparently little difference in comparative performance when the same type of ammunition is used in both weapons.

The centre-fire pistol besides being an issue to service personnel is also the weapon for police and similar organizations. Such personnel will be given training in the use of their arms for the purposes for which they will be needed and it is not the purpose of this book to describe combat shooting. It may be that in time combat shooting will take its place in civilian matches. The heavy calibre of ·45 is still used in some competitions in the U.S.A. but these are becoming fewer and the majority of civilian centre-fire shooting is with calibres of ·32 to ·38 which calibres are permitted in international competitions.

Competitions for centre fire are deliberate, timed, rapid and duelling. They will be shot on various types of target and may be akin to the military course where it is essential to fire quickly. The origin of the rapid-fire competitions came from the need to train the user of the short-barrelled weapon to be the first

CENTRE FIRE

to fire to enable him to live to fire again. The distances were short as it was not expected that the service revolver shot would have to fire his weapon at long range, but only when he was in close proximity to the enemy. It is a historic fact that few people have been known with certainty to have used a revolver in action with deadly effect. The heat of battle plays havoc with the techniques learned in the tranquillity of the training school.

The international centre-fire match consists of thirty shots deliberate and thirty shots duelling at 25 metres. The techniques for this match will be applicable to many other forms of centre-fire shooting except those which will be described later in this chapter. The deliberate course is fired in six series each of five shots and six minutes is allowed for the five shots. The targets are the same as for the 50 metres free-pistol match. A practice series of five shots is permitted and eight minutes is allowed for this. The deliberate shoot is followed by duelling at the silhouette target as used in the rapid-fire course, but each shooter has only one target. This is exposed for three seconds and turned away for seven seconds. Five shots are fired in each series and one shot is fired at each exposure.

The fundamental principles for centre-fire shooting are the same as for the small-bore pistol but two additional factors have to be taken into account. Firstly, the heavier calibre gives a stronger recoil, and secondly, the trigger must support a weight of 3 pounds.

The effect of the heavier trigger is to prolong the progressive trigger squeeze. If it is taken too quickly the shooter may not be able to judge the precise moment of release or he may tend to snatch the trigger and pull the pistol off aim. The shooter must judge the weight of the trigger and much of the weight can be taken up fairly quickly but the final let off will come at about nine seconds after the pistol is lifted to the aim. This is slightly longer than when using ·22 calibre.

The effect of recoil can be overcome with practice. The gun will have to be held very firmly and the line will have to be as straight as possible with the elbow locked. The recoil will

CENTRE FIRE

have the least effect when it can be absorbed in a straight line. Recoil has two parts, first from the ignition of the propellant and second when the bullet is released from the barrel. The first part will be when the pistol is still in the aim and if the arm is straight this will have no effect on the line of flight of the bullet. The second part will tend to throw the pistol off aim but this will not be important as the bullet will have already left the barrel. To withstand the shock of the ignition of the propellant the stance should be a little more open and the legs braced to absorb the recoil. The grip must be very firm.

The usual method of taking the grip is as follows. The instructions are for right-handed shooters. Hold the pistol round the barrel with an overhand grip with the left hand, making sure that the muzzle is not covered. Press the gun into the fork of the right hand compressing the flesh. Whilst maintaining this pressure, close the right hand round the grip making sure that the middle finger is against the trigger guard or frame, leaving the trigger finger free. Then with the thumb of left hand and a very slightly slackened grip of the right hand press in the exposed flesh round the edge of the grip before regripping tightly. Then take up the proper stance and make a practice aim squeezing the gun as hard as possible. This will cause a tremor but slacken the grip little by little until the tremor goes. This will be the firmness of grip required for centre-fire shooting. This will be learned after a time without having to go through the tremor stage. When the grip is relaxed between shots it will be just relaxed enough to allow the blood to circulate to refresh the muscles. After a centre-fire shooter has finished his shoot the firmness of grip will be shown by the marks or chequering on the surface of his hand.

As the grip has to be firm, it will quickly tire and therefore the shooter must develop the muscles to maintain this grip during training. The shooter should take the maximum time possible between shots to allow his strength to recover. The target will appear to be big at 25 metres and quite easy to hit but this is an illusion and high scores can only be obtained by hard work. The sights will be easy to see with the normal aim in the white just underneath the black. Because the aim is comparatively easy the shooter must concentrate hard to get his shot away within the time of optimum performance. If he hangs on too long to try and get a perfect shot he will find that his hand will become tired and start to tremble. This is the time to come down and rest the hand for a moment and then start again, remembering to release the trigger completely before lowering the arm.

The duelling shoot demands a change from the deliberate technique to that of snap shooting. This course takes its name, duelling, from the gallery type of shooting that followed the demise of duelling between persons. It was usual when persons were duelling for the referee to give the participants three seconds to fire their shot. There were of course many codes of rules applicable to duelling but the three-seconds rule was common to most. If the participant had not shot within that time he was not permitted to fire. This precluded a very deliberate aim being taken and gave the opponent some chance to escape being killed. The three-seconds rule has now been incorporated in the rules of this match and if the shooter does not fire his shot within this time he does not get another opportunity and loses ten points.

Not only does he have to fire within this time, but to make a good score he has to hit the target in the 10 ring, without the benefit of an aiming mark. He must give himself as much time as possible to get a good aimed shot. To do this he must first take up the proper stance so that when he lifts the pistol it will come up naturally along a vertical line through the centre of the target. The shooter must practise this time and time again until he is sure of his stance. The shooter must not lift his arm above a 45-degree angle to the horizontal or let his pistol lift off the bench until the target has commenced to turn. Then he has three seconds to lift, steady and fire. The lift should occupy about 0·8 seconds which gives him ample time (2·2 seconds) to aim and fire.

When the series commences the range officer will call 'Load'. He will then ask in a loud voice: 'Are you ready?' If there is no response he will signal the targets away. The first exposure

CENTRE FIRE

will follow in about ten seconds and thereafter the interval between exposures will be seven seconds. The shooter must learn to judge the intervals (many count the seconds) as he does not want to remain tense the whole time. He should be in the right position and when there is about four seconds to go he will glance along his pistol to see that the hand is gripping the gun at the right angle, and tighten his grip. He will then look back at the target and begin to take the progressive trigger pressure. As the targets commence to turn he will look down his sights and concentrate on getting them in the proper relationship as the arm comes up, slowing down his lift as he approaches the 8 ring and bringing the gun to a stationary position at his aiming point. He then steadies the aim and continues the trigger pressure to get a smooth let off whilst he holds a good aim. He has ample time to do this.

There is one point to remember here. If the shooter takes a '6 o'clock' aim at the deliberate target and a centre aim at the silhouette then he must alter his sights before the practice string and he should keep a permanent record in his shooting box of the normal alteration he makes. It is preferable, however, to keep the same sight-setting for both courses and in this case the aim on the silhouette target will be at about the figure '9' underneath the centre of the target. As the scoring area of the '10' is large by comparison with the precision target the shooter has a larger margin of error and provided the sight-relation picture is correct and the trigger squeeze is perfect the shot must be near the centre. The aim on the silhouette target must be consistent and the shooter will learn how far to lift his arm. He should keep his concentration on his sights and not look at the target. Immediately after he has shot he should come down and momentarily relax his hand in the grip. If he is using a revolver he will probably prefer to use it single action and cock it as soon as he comes down.

In each course of fire the shooter is allowed a practice string. In the deliberate course he is allowed eight minutes to fire the five rounds. It is important that in the first place the shooter should know his normal sight-setting for the course and see that his sights are set to this before commencing the practice, and in the second place that he should know what any alteration to his sights means on the target. He can then fire the practice with effect. The first two shots will be fired to check the conditions and to see if any alteration of sight-setting is required. The remaining three shots will be fired to build up confidence and concentration. Ample time should be taken between each shot to make sure that they are fired as near perfectly as possible.

One practice string of five rounds is allowed for the duelling course. The shooter should know if he requires any alteration to his sights for this course and he should see that he makes this before he starts his practice. He will have already fired the precision course and will be aware of the conditions. The main purpose of this practice is to confirm his natural rhythm for this course.

The shooter is allowed to spot each shot in the precision course but may not use a telescope during the firing of any string in the duelling course nor receive any directions from an assistant.

In service-type competitions, rapid fire forms the major part of the events. Under some rules the pistol used must be the type issued to the service to which the shooter belongs. It is normal for the pistol to be used as issued without alteration to the sights or grip. It is not suggested that the shooter draws a pistol from the armoury immediately before the match. He should have the opportunity of practising with it and ensuring that it is in perfect mechanical condition.

An example of the present type of British Service competition is the firing of six shots, three at each of two targets at 10 yards in six seconds. If the shooter is using a 9-millimetre Browning then he will only have to contend with holding the gun against the relatively heavy recoil of the 9-millimetre cartridge. If, on the other hand, he is using a ·380 revolver 'double action', he will have to contend with the long trigger pull which firstly has to revolve the chamber and then bring the cocking piece back against the main spring before the trigger can be released. The

CENTRE FIRE

recoil of the ·380 cartridge is much lighter than that from the 9-millimetre cartridge. If the shooter is really expert he can use his revolver 'single action' in which he cocks the hammer with the thumb of the hand holding the pistol, thereby obtaining a very crisp trigger action. If he is not such an expert shooter then he will have to speed up the action of his trigger finger so that he does not lose time. The size of the scoring zones on the target takes account of the fact that the group is likely to be fairly large and in many cases six hits on the target within the 3 zone will be quite a good score.

The pistol, whether semi-automatic or revolver, will be held in the aiming position throughout the shoot and this requires quite a degree of strength if the shooter hopes to maintain some degree of steadiness. The pistol will normally be cocked at the beginning of the shoot and therefore the first shot can be fired within the first second, this means that the following shots can be fired at intervals of just over one second. The shooter will allow himself 0·5 seconds for the gun to resettle on aim after recoil during which time he will be taking up as much of the trigger weight as he can. He can then have another half second to steady his aim before firing. The shooter will have to practise this as often as he can and if he is not shooting with live ammunition he can dry practise. This type of shoot must be planned in the same way as any other shoot and the plan rehearsed. The shooter will then come to the match knowing exactly what he has to do and the short time limit imposed will not cause him any anxiety. If he has not practised then he will be unable to judge the time and will shoot to get his shots away regardless of the score.

Dry practice will give the shooter the timing for rapid fire or duelling shooting but he will find it difficult to simulate the effect of recoil. He can to some extent simulate this by deliberately throwing the pistol off aim after the shot. Dry practice can be assisted by the use of a timer or an assistant. A simple apparatus can be made for turning targets which can be erected in a few minutes. Some centre-fire pistols can be adapted by means of a tube to fire miniature calibres such as 4 millimetre

CENTRE FIRE

and these can be used safely at short distances. There is, however, no real substitute for live shooting.

One of the greatest faults in centre-fire shooting is the inclination of some shooters to anticipate the recoil and flinch as the trigger is finally released. The flinch is either a physical flinch involving the closing of the eye and tensing of the body or is manifested in the sudden twitch of the trigger instead of a smooth let off. If the shooter is under instruction then the instructor must spot the fault as early as possible. It can be demonstrated to the shooter by inserting in his ammunition cartridges which are either dummy or have had the propellant removed. As the shooter 'fires' one of these the gun will jerk forward, showing that the shooter is pushing forward at the recoil instead of letting the recoil be taken through his arm. The shooter must immediately be taken off live shooting before the fault becomes a habit, and be given periods of dry shooting to overcome the error. One of the causes of flinch is the reaction to the loud noise when the gun fires. This can be ameliorated by the use of ear plugs or muffs. It cannot be repeated too often that the ears should be protected to avoid damage.

One of the most important aspects of centre-fire shooting is the supply of ammunition. This is expensive for the civilian shooter and many shooters use reloaded ammunition. There are facilities in some countries for purchasing factory reloads. If the shooter has his own facilities for reloading then this will reduce his expenses considerably. Some clubs offer the facilities. He can probably at least double the amount of shooting for the same outlay. It is not proposed in this chapter to go into the detail of hand loading as this is dealt with at length in books devoted to that subject.

The equipment for hand loading can be obtained and also the materials but great care should be taken to see that all the appropriate safety regulations are observed. The loads must be precise and only sound cases must be used. Some shooters when hand loading prefer to reduce the charge to avoid excessive recoil but if they are shooting in matches at a high standard then they will use the best ammunition available. They should also practice

CENTRE FIRE

with this same ammunition so that they know its characteristics with the particular pistol used. Bullets, when reloading, must be of even size and weight. They can be bought ready to use or can be cast or swaged by the shooter. If the shooter does smelt his own lead then he must take care to avoid lead poisoning, both by having a high standard of personal hygiene and by having adequate ventilation in his workshop.

Reloads should only be used in the gun for which the original cartridges were designed. Accidents have happened when the wrong cartridges have been used. Many shooters using semi-automatics shoot 9-millimetre service ammunition but it should be remembered that certain types of 9-millimetre ammunition are designed for use in automatic weapons and carry a heavier load than that designed for pistols. If too heavy a load is used then the pistol can come apart whilst shooting, with damaging effect not only to the firer but also to people in the neighbourhood. It is not worth taking the risk of causing a serious accident for the sake of a few pence.

The centre-fire course may also be fired with ·22 weapons and in many countries the two types of weapon may be fired on equal terms. The centre-fire shot holes are gauged with a ·38 gauge and the ·22 holes are gauged with a ·22 gauge. As an international competition it is used as the ladies' event but the weapon is restricted to the Standard Hand Gun. This must conform to certain dimensions and may be shot with a trigger weight not less than 1 kilogram. It is a very popular competition and will take its place among the world events. The techniques are as described for the full calibre event except that the gun will not be gripped quite so tightly nor will the trigger require so long to pull off. The standard hand gun has been introduced so that more shooters could shoot this type of competition without having the expense of the centre-fire ammunition.

The duelling part of the centre-fire event is fired with ·22 pistols as the shooting event of the modern pentathlon competition. It is surprising that higher scores are not made in this event as the participants are in the peak of physical condition. It may be that having trained for events of movement it is difficult to concentrate in a position of complete physical repose. Participants in this event would improve their scores if they undertook dry practice to give them the rhythm of firing and if they followed the suggestions given in this chapter for the centre-fire duelling course.

Another method of firing the duelling course which has been used by top shooters is to adopt a slow rhythm using the whole time available instead of firing five separate shots. When the targets turn for the first shot the pistol is brought up through the centre line of the target slowing almost to a stop just before the trigger is released and then allowing the follow through to continue up through the target to a point above the aiming mark. The pistol is then brought down slowly and deliberately through the centre line of the target to just below the 45° angle. This will take about six seconds from the release of the shot. The movement is then reversed and the arm will be at the 45° angle ready to start the upward movement as the targets turn. As this is repeated for each shot the whole series becomes a continuous shoot.

13

The Open Meeting

Shooters will begin their competitions in their own club, but it is hoped that before long they will take part in competitions on other ranges. By reading shooting magazines and by talking to more experienced shots, they will learn that attending and taking part in open competitions are an important part of shooting. Even a novice shooter will be able to attend and can take part in his own class.

Open meetings must be planned well in advance. It is usual for the main national meetings to be held about the same date each year and on the same range. Other meetings of lesser importance are then planned so that they do not clash with similar meetings in neighbouring areas. Minor meetings can be advertised nationally as it is not possible for the organizer of small meetings to circularize all possible competitors. The larger regional championships should be awarded to the various areas so that dates do not clash.

Whatever the size of the meeting it must be planned in detail as far in advance as possible. Entry forms must be available in good time and contain all the information that the competitor needs. They will state if the meeting will be squadded and if competitors will shoot under their classification. If the meeting is lasting more than one day a timetable will be given. The location of the range, the extent to which accommodation, refreshments, etc. will be available will be stated as well as the prizes to be awarded. The principal officials in charge should be named as well as the rules which will apply. The most important part of the entry form as far as the competitor is concerned will be the part which he has to return to the organizer with the entry fee: the competitor must see that it reaches the organizer before the closing date.

The organizer will have to plan the actual running of the competitions. When he first decides to have the meeting he will arrange for the entry forms to be circulated and will decide on the closing date. This must not be too close to the meeting otherwise the organizer will be overwhelmed at the last minute: it must not be too early otherwise the competitors will overlook the date. Closing dates should be strictly adhered to as late entries are the bane of an organizer's life. On receipt of the entry the organizer will check the competitor's rating and then fit him into his preferential squadding as far as possible. He will either be sent a squadding list or a receipt giving his competitor's number. Early in the planning the organizer will overhaul target equipment, order adequate numbers of targets and other supplies. Surplus targets can be stored if not used. Tickets for the various classifications and competitions are prepared to be issued to each competitor when he arrives at the meeting.

The organizer has to find sufficient staff to run the ranges and officials to take charge of the various activities. Range officials must be chosen for their ability to apply the rules with tact and firmness. They must see that the competitors start their competitions at the correct time and observe the proper rules, both competition and safety. They must not, on the other hand, be too officious as such an attitude can upset the shooter who may have travelled many miles to take part in a friendly competition. However, the observance of safety rules is paramount, even if it does upset some people's feelings.

The secretarial side of meetings includes the issue of tickets, the sale of ammunition and accessories, the preparation of results and statistics. At the time that tickets are issued to competitors their weapons will be tested to see that they conform to the rules, both for trigger weight and eligibility. The statistical officer will be responsible for the supervision of target scoring. This is usually done by the collection of targets from the firing point

46. Centre Fire Duelling. Waiting for target to turn. Arm at angle of 45 degrees (W. Ward).

47. Centre Fire Duelling. Firing the shot. The firmness of the grip is quite apparent.

48. (*left*) Standard Hand Gun. The ladies shoot on equal terms with the men (Author's wife). The shooter on the right is wearing ear plugs.

49. (*right*) A target used for Centre Fire Rapid Fire. The Advancing Man comes towards the shooter.

THE OPEN MEETING

and their removal to a central office for scoring. In some competitions competitors themselves will cross score targets and agree scores on the firing point, subject to check by range officials. Scores are published as soon as possible and competitors are entitled to challenge scores if they consider they are incorrect. The target will then be rechecked on payment of a small fee which is returnable to the competitor if his challenge is upheld.

It is essential at the beginning of a meeting to appoint a range committee or jury of senior officials of the organization controlling the meeting. If there is any dispute that cannot be resolved by the range official, the range committee is empowered to resolve the position and take such action as it deems fit. For smaller meetings the national organization may appoint an observer.

The work of the organizers is not finished when the shooting has finished. Target equipment has to be put away and the range restored to its original state. Scores are checked and prize lists made up and published together with an account of the meeting. The prize distribution will take place at the conclusion of the meeting. For this prizes will have to be obtained and if there are challenge trophies these will have to be recovered from the previous year's winners well before the meeting, for engraving. If the meeting is an important one, then a prominent person will have to be approached very early on to present the prizes.

There are many other points of detail that will have to be considered by the organizer, such as notification to local authorities of a large influx of people on certain days, the display of route signs leading to the venue, the reception of important visitors and either the provision of press facilities or notification to the press of results in time for publication.

It is the organizer's responsibility to see that he has not overlooked anything that will ensure the smooth running of the meeting. The competitors have an equal responsibility. In the first place they must see that the entry forms are completed in detail and returned in ample time with the correct entry fees. The submission of late entries, besides being discourteous, throws extra work on the organizer at the time when he is most busy and may mean that the competitor has to be refused permission to enter. Many meetings have clauses in their entry forms which impose quite a heavy penalty for late entries, but this is no excuse for being late.

The competitor should study the entry form to see that he is fully conversant with all aspects of the organization and knows exactly what he has to do when he arrives at the meeting. He should prepare his equipment well in advance and make good any deficiencies. He should study the rules so that he understands all the orders he is likely to be given. The success of all meetings depends on the co-operation between the organizers and the competitors. A competitor who does not know the rules will not only be an embarrassment to the officials, but also to the other competitors.

On arrival the competitor should report to the office to check in and collect his tickets and instructions. He should take his guns with him at this time in case they are required to be controlled at this point. Before leaving the office he should check his tickets to see that he has been given them for all competitions for which he entered. He should examine the squadding list and make a note of times of details and target numbers. He should make sure that he has sufficient ammunition for the whole of the meeting and before he leaves the office he should inspect any notice boards for up-to-date information. He should then make a tour of the range so that he knows where all the facilities are situated.

When the actual time of competition is close the competitor should check his equipment and make his way to the firing point to arrive there about fifteen minutes before he is due to shoot. He can then relax for a few minutes and whilst relaxing can study the conditions and begin to plan his shoot. He will then be able to take his place on the firing point in the proper frame of mind. On the firing point the competitor will conduct himself according to the instructions of the range officer and, if in any doubt, should raise any queries with him before the match commences. He will then apply himself to the competition having resolved all his problems before the shooting begins.

If the meeting is a large one it may last several days and will attract many shooters who have to travel considerable distances. The shooter may travel with other competitors or may take his family. Besides being shooting occasions when trophies are won or lost, regional and national meetings are social occasions when old friends are met and new acquaintances are made. Competitors go to these meetings hoping to do well in competition but also intending to make them social meetings. The serious competitor must go with the intention of doing well in competition and will forego the social pleasures until the shooting is over. The big-match shot will see that he has plenty of rest and a good night's sleep. He will try and avoid those shooters who prefer to sit up half the night yarning. He will plan properly balanced meals and will find that a light meal about an hour or so before shooting will serve him much better than a heavy one. If he has to travel a long way he will try and do his journey the day before the meeting. The strain of driving long distances is quite considerable, both physically and mentally. Some shooters do manage to drive and shoot, but as a general rule it is not wise.

Whether the competitor is a serious shooter or not, he will enjoy the friendly atmosphere of the big meeting. He will have the opportunity to see the top shooters in action and see a far greater variety of equipment than if he did not venture away from his own range.

So far the accent has been on the individual but in many matches the team is more important than the individual and the individual must be prepared to subordinate his own identity to becoming a competent team member. Team matches can be roughly split into two categories. There are the teams that are formed from members who have entered the competitions as individuals and where the team shoot is concurrent, and the matches where teams shoot shoulder to shoulder.

In the first category an official will be appointed to pick the team virtually on the spot. This may be a club team entry and the team captain will have some idea who will be entering but he will delay his selection until the last moment to find out who is on form. All potential members of a team should know that

THE OPEN MEETING

they are being considered for selection and this should be a spur to greater effort as it is an honour to be selected for a team.

Where teams are selected for shoulder-to-shoulder matches the selectors should endeavour to pick shooters who will rise to the occasion as good team shooters. If possible they should get together as much as possible before the match so that they know each other and their officials. In some competitions teams can be selected and trained well before the matches.

This chapter has been designed to give shooters some ideas about open meetings, not only for their own benefit but to show that the organizers have to undertake a great amount of work long before a shot is fired. One often hears criticism of the running of meetings but if the competitors stopped to think for a moment, then they would realize that the meetings are organized for their benefit and that is the purpose of the organization. Shooting organizations welcome constructive criticism and many improvements have been incorporated based on suggestions from competitors.

14

International Meetings

The major international shooting organization is the Union International de Tir which has its headquarters in Wiesbaden, West Germany. It has a permanent secretariat but its council and specialist committees are made up of representatives from many nations. The U.I.T. is responsible for the organization, in conjunction with the national organization of the host nation, of the major international events such as World Championships, World Regional Championships and Olympic Games. It caters for all types of shooting, small-bore and full-bore rifle, small-bore and full-bore pistol, sporting rifle, trap and skeet, air rifle and air pistol. The competitions held under U.I.T. rules are defined and are limited so that all nations know that they can train their shooters under the same rules as all other nations. The rules and competitions are kept up to date with current thought in shooting and proposals which come from the Technical or Executive Committees are published in the journal of the organization, *Shooting Sport*.

The holding of an international meeting is a tremendous undertaking and the preparation can start years ahead. Technical Committees examine the suggested venues for ranges and plans are submitted. Ranges must conform to certain standards in construction and must be large enough to accommodate the shooting of any one competition in any one day apart from the Rapid-Fire Pistol event which is frequently spread over two days. This generally means that for the rifle and free-pistol shooting there must be at least a hundred targets at 50 metres and for the rapid fire at least twelve sets of silhouette targets at 25 metres. These are the requirements for pistol shooting and there are the other events to be included. Different venues may cater for different aspects of the sport but they will be reasonably close for administrative reasons. Plans will have to be made for accommodating the large influx of competitors and officials and the provision of such ancillary services as transport and interpreters. Some wonderful ranges have been built for international competitions, and Bucharest, Cairo, Caracas, Tokyo and Wiesbaden are but a few. The cost of providing such ranges is very high indeed, running into hundreds of thousands of pounds. This cost cannot be borne by the shooting organizations alone and considerable assistance is given from government subsidies and philanthropic sources. Once built, however, they are an asset to the national organization.

The detailed running of the meetings has to be carefully studied and rehearsed. Owing to the large number of shooters competing at any one time, the number of people employed as target changers, register keepers, scorers, etc. will also be large. The interest of both the shooter and spectator is stimulated by the display of current scores. One of the drawbacks to the sport of shooting is the lack of spectator appeal. Shooting is an amateur sport where the competitor is disinterested in the spectator but the sport might benefit financially if it were given more spectator appeal.

The rapid display of scores whilst the shooting is progressing allows the spectators to follow the leading shooters and the use of closed circuit television showing the targets as they are hit might attract a paying audience.

It is hoped, however, that the sport will remain permanently amateur and that the big meetings will be friendly meetings of competitors each determined to do his best but at the same time recognizing that the best man or woman on the day will be a worthy and acclaimed champion. The shooters who achieve selection for their national teams have done so through determination and hard work. Methods of selection differ from nation to nation and much depends on the number of shooters in each nation who are in the top grades and eligible for selection. There will always be discussion and argument over the best methods as there will always be those who consider that the selectors have made the wrong choice.

Whatever the methods involved the selectors must make their methods known to all concerned from the start. In the early stages the selection will be from as broad a base as possible and the unknown but promising shooter must be brought into competition with the known and established international shot. This will be a long-term process as it will be unwise to give a place to an inexperienced shot when there are established shots of equal merit.

Area trials will lead to central shoulder-to-shoulder trials and from these a small number will be selected to undergo intensive competition shooting to improve their techniques and to see if they can maintain their high scores under match pressure. The atmosphere of the big international match has to be experienced and is difficult to simulate but unless the shooter has been tried under severe pressure, he will be a doubtful candidate for selection.

The shooter must be expected to reach a certain standard laid down by the selectors before he can be considered for selection. Once this standard has been reached further selection will be on a competitive basis. The match atmosphere must be simulated as far as possible and the shooters will be expected to shoot on various ranges in the course of the trials. If possible matches should be arranged against neighbouring nations and the teams involved should be larger than the number required for the big international meeting. This will enable the selectors to bring untried shooters of the necessary potential into the team. This will serve two purposes; firstly it will put pressure on the established shooter to work hard to keep his place in the team, and secondly it will enable the potential of the untried shooter to be tested in the right atmosphere. The national organizations should see that they give their best shooters the facilities and opportunities to give of their best.

The function of the team manager is very important and he

INTERNATIONAL MEETINGS

may have to act as team coach if a coach is not separately appointed. It is the responsibility of the team officials to see that the team arrives on the firing point determined to win. Each shooter has a different personality but it will be the function of the team official to know each member of his team and all his idiosyncracies so that whatever the situation the official will know exactly how each member of the team will react. To take the extremes, one shooter will shoot best if he is left entirely alone whilst another needs constant fussing. The manager must exercise discipline over the team, but must know how each member will react to his supervision. The team members, on the other hand, know that they are representing their nation and must respect the decisions of the officials in charge. The shooters should be given all information that is available as early as possible and team officials should be available for advice at any reasonable time. This will allow a good team spirit to be built up. This team spirit can be developed if regular team meetings are held; this is made easier if all the team is accommodated together.

The conduct of the big international match will probably be strange to many shooters. Shooting is done to strict timetables. Targets are allocated to nations for practice before the day of the match. It could be that owing to the large number of competitors practice facilities may seem to be inadequate. These conditions will apply to all nations and it is up to the team manager to make his own timetable for his team's practice. This should be done with each member of the team in mind as some may require more practice than others. It may be possible to enlist the aid of local clubs but all members must have some experience on the match range. Competitors not actually shooting practice should be encouraged to assist those on the firing point to enable both firer and non-firer to familiarize himself with the range conditions.

The day of arrival at an international meeting will probably be confusing to the newcomer. Team officials will be visiting the various offices to gather all the information they can and to collect any official documents that may have to be distributed to members of the team. Competitors will have to check in their weapons for official approval and will have an official seal affixed. Unless that seal is on the weapon it will not be permitted to be used in the match. Competitors will have a general look round the facilities and will gather together at some suitable time for a briefing by the team manager.

There are likely to be official receptions and visits to places of interest. Whilst every advantage should be taken of sight-seeing, such activities must be considered in the light of the shooting programme and care taken that the shooter does not become overtired before he has completed his shooting programme. Whilst visiting foreign cities the team will, in the eyes of the host nation and the local inhabitants, be the representatives of the nation which has sent them. It is only common courtesy to respect the wishes and customs of the local people and such courtesy will make a lasting impression.

Trips abroad tend to upset the normal functions of the body unless prior precautions are taken. The competitors should have been advised before departure if any special medication to combat the ill effects of strange foods and water is needed. It is much better to take these precautions than have to suffer not only physically but subsequent loss of form. Strange foods should be avoided unless the visitor has had previous experience of them.

The evening before the match the competitor should carefully check his equipment and make sure that his pistol is in perfect condition. The team manager or coach will advise him of any last-minute details and tell him the number of the target and time of shoot. Where the team match is based on the aggregate of the scores in the individual match the team may find itself split up along the range. It may happen that the match will be fired in more than one detail and in this case the team will be split. The organizers try and equalize the advantages and disadvantages of position and time by allocating targets in various parts of the firing point, so that the team as a whole has the same conditions as all other teams. It may be that because of this the individual does not get the most favourable position.

INTERNATIONAL MEETINGS

Target allocations are made by lottery in the presence of team officials. It will be the responsibility of the official in charge of the team to allocate the times and targets to his team. He will do this in the light of his knowledge of each shooter. Normally shooters are squadded in pairs and if in the morning detail two targets are allocated on the left of the range, then in the afternoon they will be at the right-hand end of the range. This will only occur when there are insufficient targets for all competitors to fire in one detail. With rapid fire and centre fire the shooter will be allocated to one stand for the first half of the shoot and to another for the second half.

Shooting will be timed to give the shooters as far as possible the best possible conditions. It may be that owing to heat and humidity during the middle part of the day, shooting will commence very early and then cease for several hours during the middle of the day. The competitor must be aware of such timing and must as far as possible practise at the same time as he will shoot in the match. Competitors should reach their appointed firing point in plenty of time so that they can set up their equipment and have time to sit down before the shooting begins.

The Free-Pistol Match and the other pistol events differ in their procedure and in the first place the detail of the Free-Pistol Match will be described. Each shooter will have his own target which will be plainly numbered. Behind each shooter will be a register keeper. He will be responsible for keeping a register of the signalled scores where butt marking is used and also to signal to the marker when the shot has been fired. The register keeper may be a serviceman, a local volunteer or a member of a rifle or pistol club. He may or may not speak the same language as the shooter, but the shooter will have to communicate with him from time to time. The range will be divided into sections each in charge of an official. These officials will have distinguishing badges as will also the members of the controlling organization who will constantly patrol the range generally to observe the conduct of the shooters and to resolve any difficulties that may arise. It is very important that the competitors are fully conversant with the rules as failure to observe them in detail can result in the shooter being penalized. On one occasion at a recent international meeting a change in rules was announced over the public address system five minutes before the match commenced. The controlling officials can examine clothing and equipment but do not usually interrupt the shooter during the competition to do so. Checks are normally made during the practice periods and any shooter who thinks that some of his equipment may be questioned should take it to the equipment control office well before the match. If it does not comply with the rules he still has time to change it or alter it before the match.

The register keeper will have a board showing the name of the shooter and also a book or pad for sending back provisional scores to the score board. The competitor should check that the register keeper has the right name. The shooter will then set up his equipment and can fire a few warming-up shots when permitted to do so. A few minutes before the scheduled time of the start a further announcement will be made that warming-up shots must cease. This announcement as well as any others on the range will be given in the official languages for the meeting. As the time of the start draws near, a hush comes over the range as shooters begin their final preparations. The experienced shooter will have already completed his and will be sitting quietly on his chair mentally composing himself for the match. He will be watching the conditions and from his knowledge gained during the practice periods will have made his plan. As the hand of the clock comes up to the scheduled time the public address system will announce the commencement of the match and the targets will appear. The first target up will be the practice target. This is normally distinguished by having a black stripe across one corner. All the shooter's practice shots will be on this target. Before starting to shoot the competitor should examine his target to see that it does not have any blemishes and that it does have his target number written on it. This can be seen through the telescope. The competitor should have been issued with two discs on sticks which he can show to the register keeper. One disc will indicate that he wishes to shoot practice shots and the other that he is shooting match shots. So to begin with he will hold up the practice disc and commence shooting.

Most international ranges have markers' galleries and the value of each shot is signalled from the butts by the target operator. A shot having been fired, the register keeper will wait for a few seconds to allow the shooter to spot it through his telescope and will then signal to the butts, normally by means of a push button, that a shot has been fired. The marker will dip the target and on re-exposing it will indicate by international code the value of the shot and its position. He will have also placed a transparent patch over it so that any shot going close to a previous one will perforate the transparent patch and its position will be obvious. Once the shooter has completed his practice shots he will indicate to the register keeper that he wishes his first match card to go up. The register keeper will signal the butts to this effect and the practice target will be lowered and replaced with a match target. This will have no distinguishing marks but the shooter should examine it through the telescope to make sure that it is a clean target and that it has his target number on it and the correct consecutive number. Match targets will normally be changed every five or ten shots and removed from the butts to the target control for scoring. Although the register keeper maintains a shot by shot record of the score as indicated by the marker, the official score is taken from the target by the Classing Committee. The competitor should take careful note of any doubtful shots so that he can make sure that the official score is correct. The register keeper should delay signalling that a shot has been fired until the shooter has indicated that this can be done. If the target is being dipped too quickly then the shooter should either ask his team manager or official to ask the range official to instruct the register keeper accordingly, or he can do so himself.

The competitor may return to his practice card only between ten-shot series unless shooting is interrupted through outside causes. The rules allow for additional practice shots if shooting is held up for any length of time. Shooting will be continuous throughout the time of the match and competitors are at liberty to leave the range if they so wish. They are not allowed, however, to receive direct coaching instructions. They may approach their team officials on matters relating to the rules. At the end of the time allowed for the match an announcement will be made and the targets lowered. It is desirable that the competitor should be assisted behind the firing point by another team member or official. If he is in any trouble or if he needs any advice other than coaching advice, he should be able to turn at once to an assistant. His gun may go wrong and he may need an armourer's assistance to put it right. He may have a point to raise concerning his target or an official may approach him regarding an item of his equipment. The team official is there to help and assist him in every respect. The shooter is on the firing point to do his best and he should therefore not have to worry about anything else. He expects the other team members not shooting and the team officials to do the worrying for him if anything goes wrong. This applies to all competitions and not only to Free Pistol.

When the competitor has finished his match he should remain quiet until his neighbours have finished their next shot before he packs up his equipment and leaves the firing point. He will check his score with the register keeper who will give him a copy of the board score for later comparison with the official score. The shooter will also have kept his own shot-by-shot diagram and will know whether the register keeper has kept a correct record although this is unimportant. The targets are continuously scored by the members of the Classing Committee throughout the competition and the final results are entered on the scoring board shortly after the end of the match.

There is one aspect of the Free Pistol match that should be brought to the attention of all shooters. Until recently if the pistol was fired whilst any part of it was still in contact with the bench or table on the firing point, the shooter was permitted another shot even if the accidental discharge had hit the target. This accidental shot was discounted. The rule was difficult to apply as it was not easy for the range official to determine whether the gun was on the bench or just off it when the accidental discharge occurred. The register keeper would not normally see the shooter's action at the time being positioned directly behind him and the range officials are not able to watch every firer at the same time. The rule was therefore amended in 1966 and accidental discharge now incurs a penalty. The accidental discharge now counts if it hits any part of the target, even the non-scoring part. If there is no hit on the target then the shooter is permitted another shot but is penalized 2 points. Shooters who use very light triggers must take great care when setting the trigger and when lifting the pistol to the aim and all shooters will now have to take care over the handling of the pistol whilst on the bench.

There will be quite a number of spectators behind the firing point, members of the public as well as other competitors. They will initially gather behind the better-known shots and there will also be a small crowd behind the shooters from the host nation. When any shooter is in sight of a high score, the news will rapidly spread and he will attract the greatest number of spectators. The established international shot will have become accustomed to shooting in front of a crowd of people but it may affect neighbouring less-experienced shooters. The spectators will discuss each shot, will lean forward and take photographs and generally be a distraction. If, however, the competitors are wearing ear muffs the noises will be subdued and if the spectators are talking in an unfamiliar language then in all probability the shooter will ignore the noise. The successful shooter has had to learn to overcome the noises behind him and concentrate entirely on the shooting. It is probable that unless the shooter looks round he is unaware of the crowd behind him. The top shooter is successful because he is able to ignore all outside influences when concentrating on the task in hand.

The majority of spectators will concentrate their attentions on the more spectacular events—the rapid-fire and centre-fire pistol matches. The crowds will be very large behind the more eminent shooters. The excitement can be intense towards the end of a shoot when a high score is possible. The effect on the rapid-fire shooter, however, can be far greater than on the free-

INTERNATIONAL MEETINGS

pistol shooter as the rapid-fire shooter has no chance of recovery if his concentration is diverted.

The routine for the shooters in these events will follow a similar pattern to that which has been described for the free-pistol shooter. Training periods will be allotted to the various national teams and it is the duty of the team officials to see that these times are utilized to the full. If the entry list is very full it may mean that very early starts will have to be made, as this type of range accommodation is generally inadequate. Training will take place on the same ranges as used for the match so that competitors will have experience of the target equipment and the conditions. The actual match will be run to a very strict timetable and the shooter will not be allowed on the firing point until he is called forward. He will then take up his stand on the firing point and prepare himself and his equipment for the event. The allocation of shooters to the allotted firing stands will be at the discretion of the team official.

Each range will be in charge of a range officer and he will have an operator to control the working of the targets. In addition to a member of the Classing Committee there will also be a member of the Jury of Appeal in attendance to resolve any difficulties on the spot. The shooter will show the range officer that his weapon conforms to the rules governing dimensions and weight. The testing equipment will be on the firing point. Having completed these formalities, the shooter will indicate which time duration he wishes for the practice series. The range officer will test the operation of the targets and check the timing with a stop watch and will then wait for the shooter to indicate that he is ready. This will be done verbally by the shooter. The range officer will then signal the operator to work the targets and the shooter will fire without any further word of command as soon as the targets face towards him.

It is usual to have two sets of silhouette apparatus under the control of one official and one operator and one team of markers. Shooters will therefore be on the firing point in pairs and they fire each series alternately. When they come to fire the second thirty-shot course the shooters will change positions as well as fire on a different stand. After both shooters have fired one five-shot series the targets will be faced and the scoring team will score the targets. This team usually consists of a marker and a caller who may also insert a coloured spotting disc into the shot hole. The caller will also call the value of the shot. If a score is in doubt the member of the Classing Committee will decide the value of the shot with a gauge before the coloured disc is inserted into the shot hole. The caller is followed by his assistant who will remove the marking discs and will cover each shot hole with a transparent paper wafer. The marker will also record each shot on the score sheet and will call out the total value of the five-shot series for an assistant on the firing point to chalk up on a board at the firing point. Each series will be fired in the same way until the thirty-shot course is completed. The total score will then be displayed and the shooter will pack up his equipment and leave the firing point.

He will fire the second half course according to the timetable. If there is a big entry and insufficient sets of target apparatus the match may last two days. If on the first day he fired in the morning then on the second day he will fire in the afternoon and vice versa. As far as possible all shooters are given as near equal conditions as possible.

In the centre-fire match the precision course will be fired by all competitors before the duelling course commences. This latter shoot can be most economical of range space as five shooters can be accommodated on each set of target apparatus whereas only two could shoot rapid fire. The silhouette targets will have been taken out of their frames and replaced with the precision targets as the match will be shot on the same range as the rapid-fire match. Nations will have been allocated targets by lot as usual and each member of the team will probably find himself on a different range, and, if there is more than one detail, at different starting times. Partitions will have been fixed between one shooter and the next to give neighbouring shooters some protection from the elements and also from ejected cartridge cases. Guns will be inspected by the range officer before the match both for dimensions and for trigger weight. When the range officer considers that the shooters are ready to start he will give the order to commence the practice target, five shots in eight minutes. When this has finished the match targets will be fired in series of five shots in six minutes on each target. They may be scored on the range and the scores chalked up for the information of the firers and spectators or they will be removed to the Classing Committee for scoring. The shooters will know their own scores as they will have been spotting each shot and will have kept a shot-by-shot record.

When the duelling course takes place a single silhouette target will have been put up opposite each firer and on taking his position on the range the shooter will again have his pistol tested. He will then prepare himself for the course and all competitors on that part of the range will shoot together. The range officer will wait until all shooters are apparently ready to shoot and he will then call: 'Are you ready?' (This order will be given in one of the official languages of the U.I.T.) If there is no reply to this order, the official will by the rules assume that all shooters are ready and will signal the operator to operate the targets. When each series of five shots has been fired the targets will be scored. This will be done in a way similar to the rapid-fire scoring but in this case there is one target with five shots per shooter. The shots will be called from the lowest to the highest and will also be called in the official language being used. If the shooter had 3 × 10, 1 × 9 and 1 × 8, he will hear EIGHT, NINE, TEN, TEN, TEN. TOTAL FORTY-SEVEN. The shot holes will be indicated by coloured discs, red ones being used for tens and white ones for other values. Targets or target centres will be changed so that the scores can be checked by the Classing Committee. All shot holes will be gauged with the ·38 or metric equivalent gauge irrespective of the size of calibre used by the competitor which may be between 7·65 millimetres and 9 millimetres. When the shooting has finished the competitor will pack up his equipment and leave the firing point.

It will be noted that there has been no mention of inspection of pistols on the firing point to see that they are left in a safe condition. Shooters in the international class are expected to be fully conversant with the rules concerning safety and are expected to comply with them without supervision. The shooter engaged in rapid fire or centre fire will lay his weapon on the table as soon as he has finished a five-shot series and will not touch it again until ordered to load or reload. He will himself see that the pistol is clear before he leaves the firing point.

When matches are completed victory ceremonies are held. Congratulations are given to the winners by all and sundry. It has been said that the winners are the shooters with the luck. This may be true to some extent: the winner may well be the one who had his shots just on the line whilst the loser had them just out. However, whoever wins a big competition is always a worthy winner. International meetings are very friendly affairs and whilst there is tremendous rivalry on the firing point, and often some argument with officials over points of procedure, there is never animosity. Shooters mix freely with one another and conduct conversations without knowing more than a few words of one another's language. They have a common language, the intense interest in shooting. These meetings open and close with impressive ceremonies and there is usually some central celebration where the shooters relax in congenial surroundings. After all the shooting is over, farewells are said and shooters return to their own countries, hoping that the opportunity will come to them again to compete for the highest honours.

15

Coaching

Pistol coaching, either individual or team, is a very difficult task and coaches must possess certain attributes. They do not necessarily have to be highly skilled shots, but must have experience and complete knowledge of the techniques.

The coach must also have patience—patience to stand with the skilled shot for a long time analysing his shooting and giving him constructive advice. He must be enthusiastic and be able to persuade the most temperamental shooter that he should take a certain course of action. He must have personality and self-assurance so that the shooters will respect him and follow his directions without question.

At the club level the coach will also be the instructor who will give the novice his first knowledge of the pistol and then guide his progress until he is a top club shooter. If the shooter has been properly trained he will not be satisfied that he has reached the peak of his potential by shooting only for his club. The club instructor will see that the shooter is passed on to the expert coaches who must be able to bring out the best in any shooter.

Most nations have in existence, or are bringing into being, national coaching schemes. This ensures that in the first place coaches receive uniform instruction and secondly that there are facilities to coach the potential top-class shooter. Regular courses should be run by the national coaches for regional coaches who in turn will run courses for county and club coaches. Club coaches will, of course, be given the opportunity to attend central courses as well as county courses. The higher the general standard of the coaches the higher will be the standard of shooting. Coaches or potential coaches who attend courses must be examined and if successful be given a qualification. The national coaches besides running the regional courses will be responsible for seeing that the standard of coaching is maintained and will also be responsible for the national team training. The coaching training scheme will fall under the direction of the national civilian shooting organization whilst the services will organize their own shooting schools. The means may be different but the ends should be the same, a general improvement in the standard of shooting and the discovery and proper training of potential top shooters. In the services the potential shooter can be directed to be sent on specialized courses to develop his skills and if suitable to become an instructor. The civilian has to find the time to take training courses and it will not be so easy for him. He will, however, probably have the greater initial enthusiasm to encourage him to overcome his difficulties.

The task of the club coach will be twofold. Firstly he will have to instruct the novices and secondly he will have to coach the trained shot. He will usually be a shooter who would rather undertake this task than be a shooting team member and it will take up as much of his time as he can spare. The coach will lay down a training programme which he will expect the trainee shooter to follow. The programme will not only lay down each stage of the learning process but will also be a timetable. It will be the instructor's responsibility to see that a group of novices are brought along together, instead of having a new one turning up every week so that the class never get beyond lesson 1! The coach will see that the programme is as broadly based as possible and will make sure that the pupils undertake to participate in the whole of the programme and not select some parts to suit themselves.

The coach will take the shooter through the various courses of fire and when he has completed the courses the coach will give him a test and a qualification. He will then be in a position to have individual coaching to improve his techniques and to eliminate his errors. This is where the knowledge and experience of the coach can be of immense assistance. He must know exactly what the shooter is doing and will watch him for some time before making any recommendation. The shooter must be absolutely honest in his dealing with his coach as unless the coach gets true answers to his questions he cannot hope to give the shooter proper advice. The coach will question the shooter after each shot and the shooter should not have the use of a telescope whilst under instruction. The coach will ask the shooter to describe exactly what he felt about each shot or each series of shots so that he can have the shooter's opinion to compare with his own assessment. Very often it is by discussion of a problem with an experienced coach that the answer is forthcoming. Once the coach has come to a decision that the shooter is committing an error he must tell the shooter what he is doing wrong and what he must do to apply the correct technique. He cannot insist that the shooter follows his advice but the shooter will be wasting his own time as well as that of the coach if he does not. The shooter will also find that the coach will be loathe to offer him any further advice if he is not prepared to follow it.

The club coach will have his eye on any potential top-grade shooter and see that he gets the opportunity to gain more experience. Club coaches should attend meetings at which club members or teams are competing.

By the operation of a coaching system, the potential top-class shots will be brought to the notice of the national coaches and central shooting courses may be held from time to time to improve the techniques of the top shooters. The national coaches will get to know the individuals who make up the basis of the national teams. Each individual will have to be treated in the most suitable manner and it is the responsibility of the experienced coach to know how to get the best performance from the individual. He will have to instil into the shooter that he is being coached to win, either as an individual or as a member of a team. The coach must study the national team shooters while they are shooting so that he learns their individual techniques. He can then spot when they are making errors and advise

COACHING

how they should eradicate their faults. The shooter should never be destructively criticized for bad shooting but should always be encouraged to produce a better performance.

At the time of the match the coach will be present to see to the detailed arrangements. He will ensure that his team arrives on the firing point fully prepared and confident to give of their collective best. This will be due to the personality of the coach having instilled into the team a feeling of mutual respect and confidence. The coach will have given praise for a job well done, listened sympathetically to the shooter who has had a bad shoot without condemning him, and quietly encouraged him to believe that he can do a little better. If the coach has done his job properly there should seldom be any failure on the part of the shooter.

During the match he will be in attendance, to give technical assistance if the rules permit coaching. Otherwise he will watch the shooters with a critical eye and note any points that are worthy of discussion at a later time. He will watch the activities of the officials and see that the team members are not interrupted during the shooting. He will be a ready listener when his team have finished the match.

The ability of a good coach is shown by the improved performance of the individual or team which he has been coaching. Any improvement is only achieved by hard work both by the coach and by the shooters. The personal example of the coach is extremely important. He will be as enthusastic and cheerful at the end of a training session as he was at the beginning. Enthusiasm is infectious and even though the coach will impose discipline, his leadership will ensure that his requests are cheerfully and willingly observed.

APPENDIX A

Exercises

The following exercise programme is reproduced by permission of the Commanding Officer, United States Army Advanced Marksmanship Training Unit, Georgia, U.S.A.

D. THE SEVENTY-SECOND FORMULA

The Pistol Division of the United States Army Marksmanship Training Unit is presently using a series of dynamic tension physical exercises. These exercises were described in outline by a Canadian Army Captain while attending one of the Advanced Pistol Marksmanship Courses conducted by U.S.A.M.T.U. Pistol Division.

According to a report from the Canadian Army, an experiment was conducted at the University of British Columbia utilizing two groups, one group performed the new tension exercises while the other performed more vigorous exercises utilizing weights, etc. for a period of sixty days. At the end of this sixty-day period the group performing the tension exercises doubled their strength while the other group experienced no great physical improvement.

In view of these reported results the fact that pistol shooters require physical stamina to perform efficiently, the minimum time required to perform the exercises, the absence of danger of strained muscles and injuries, the SEVENTY-SECOND exercises has been adopted and is used by all members of the U.S.A.M.T.U. Pistol Group for testing and reported results.

EXERCISES

How to do them

One of the great advantages of this programme is that no special equipment is required. The exercises can be performed at any time when seventy seconds can be spared. It is suggested however that a routine time such as when arising in the morning be selected.

The main thing is EFFORT. Each exercise is performed to a count of one thousand—two thousand—three thousand—four thousand—five thousand—six thousand, etc., pressure or stretching being applied to the full throughout the count. Part of the theory is that a muscle builds more rapidly under tension applied vigorously for a short period than it can when put to use over a prolonged period. The latter results in a build-up of lactic acid (a product of exertion) which finally becomes so accumulated within the fibres of the muscles that further movement is impossible until the acid has been absorbed into the system.

The exercises

EXERCISE 1

Hands held fingers up, finger tips in line with chin, elbows raised in line with shoulders. Hands pressed one against the other with as much effort as possible.

PUSH → ← PUSH HERE

EXERCISE 2

Both hands gripped at waist level, as much effort as possible exerted in squeezing hands together.

SQUEEZE

EXERCISE 3

Arms hanging loose slightly bent in front of body, palm of

EXERCISES

hand facing forward. Suddenly and with as much squeeze as possible contract the bicep and clench the fists tight.

EXERCISE 4
Arms loose at sides. Suddenly extend arms backwards as high as possible, fingers stiff, whole arm as tense as possible.

EXERCISE 5
Arms extended over head in relaxed position. Suddenly make every effort to force finger tips through ceiling.

EXERCISE 6
Arms extended in front of body. Suddenly try to force arms with outstretched fingers through opposite wall.

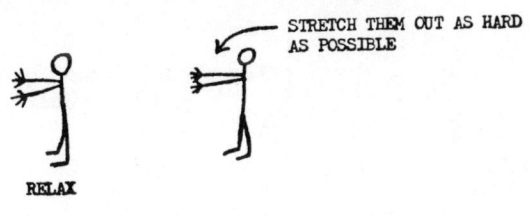

EXERCISES

EXERCISE 7

Hands on hips, weight normal on balls of feet. Suddenly tense arms, abdomen and all leg muscles.

TENSE EVERYTHING YOU CAN

RELAX

EXERCISE 8

Sit on floor legs crossed, arms at sides. Suddenly bend toes inward towards heel, tense leg muscles.

CURL INWARDS, WORK AT IT!!

RELAX

EXERCISE 9

Lie on floor face down. Suddenly arch backwards; try to touch head to heels. Arms extended backwards and up.

This is one that is guaranteed to reduce pant size from 38 inches to 28 inches!

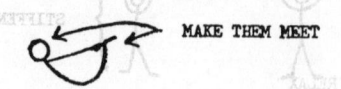

MAKE THEM MEET

EXERCISE 10

Place one side against a wall, arms at sides. Suddenly stiffen side nearest wall and try to shove your way through it. Now try the other side.

STIFFEN, REACH FOR FLOOR WITH FINGERS & SHOVE

RELAX

EXERCISES

EXERCISE 11

Back to wall, fingers on collar-bone, elbows in line with shoulders. Suddenly try to shove your chin through wall opposite, at same time try to flatten shoulders against the wall behind.

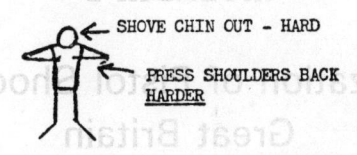

SHOVE CHIN OUT - HARD

PRESS SHOULDERS BACK **HARDER**

EXERCISE 12

Stand about 18 inches from wall. Raise the toes, stand on heels, place hand on wall for balance. Suddenly try to touch knees with toes and floor with your rear end.

PUSH EVERYTHING DOWN

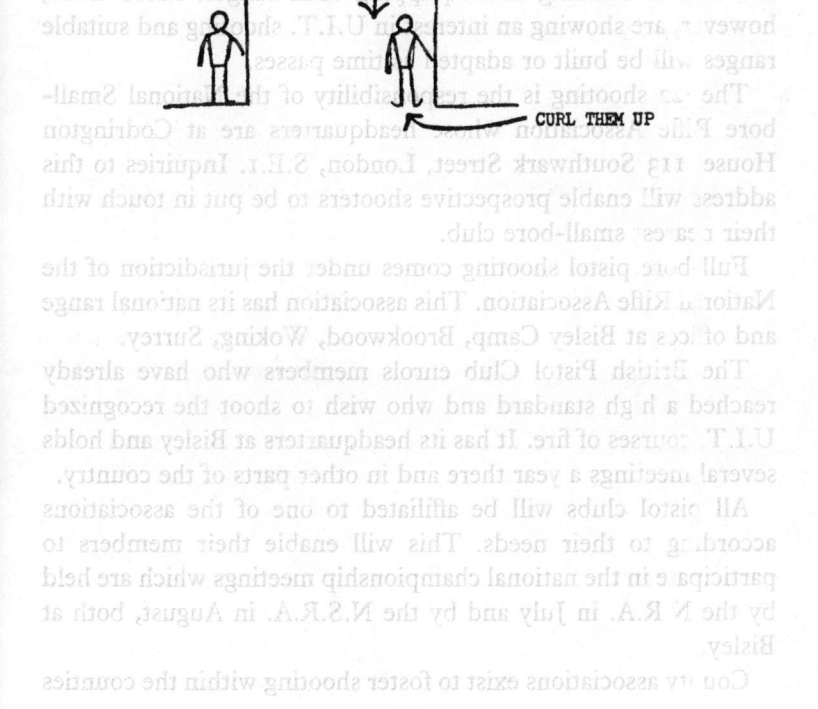

CURL THEM UP

APPENDIX B

Organization of Pistol Shooting in Great Britain

Rifle and pistol clubs exist all over Great Britain but in the main they only cater for ·22 shooting. Pistol shooting is either the sole function of the club or is a sectional interest of a rifle club. Clubs catering for centre-fire and rapid-fire silhouette shooting are few owing to the very stringent safety requirements and also the cost of building and equipping such ranges. More clubs, however, are showing an interest in U.I.T. shooting and suitable ranges will be built or adapted as time passes.

The ·22 shooting is the responsibility of the National Smallbore Rifle Association whose headquarters are at Codrington House, 113 Southwark Street, London, S.E.1. Inquiries to this address will enable prospective shooters to be put in touch with their nearest small-bore club.

Full-bore pistol shooting comes under the jurisdiction of the National Rifle Association. This association has its national range and offices at Bisley Camp, Brookwood, Woking, Surrey.

The British Pistol Club enrols members who have already reached a high standard and who wish to shoot the recognized U.I.T. courses of fire. It has its headquarters at Bisley and holds several meetings a year there and in other parts of the country.

All pistol clubs will be affiliated to one of the associations according to their needs. This will enable their members to participate in the national championship meetings which are held by the N.R.A. in July and by the N.S.R.A. in August, both at Bisley.

County associations exist to foster shooting within the counties

ORGANIZATION OF PISTOL SHOOTING IN GREAT BRITAIN

and to co-ordinate the activities of the clubs within their areas.

The national associations are responsible for selecting national teams in the disciplines they administer and for nominating to a joint shooting committee their selections for international teams.

Index

Accessories, 38–41
Accidental discharge, 125, 157
Accidents, 32, 39, 141
Aiming, 50–53, 75–83, 117, 123, 126, 137
Ammunition, 37, 38, 59, 73, 140
　service, 38, 141
　reloaded, 39, 73, 140
Arc of movement, 81

Breathing, 57, 110
British Pistol Club, 172

Cant, 81
Centre of gravity, 44, 47
Cleaning, 37, 38, 74, 101, 126
Clothing, 91, 132
Combat shooting, 19, 133
Conditioned reflex, 112, 119, 123

Diet, 89, 90
Double action, 138
Drugs, 91
Dry practice, 71, 85, 129, 139
Duelling, 136

Ear protectors, 40, 93, 132
Ears, care of, 92
Electric trigger, 102
Exercise, 88, 89
Eye, dominant, 52, 53
Eyes, care of, 91, 92
Eyesight, defective, 52, 92

Firearms certificate, 21
Firing pin, 32, 60
Flinch, 85, 140
Follow through, 54, 56, 127
Footwear, 43

Grip, 45 et seq, 49, 83
　centre fire, 135
　free pistol, 103
　rapid fire, 118, 130
Group, 64, 65, 75, 81, 103, 120, 131

Handgun, standard, 141
Hand loading, 39, 73, 140

Line of sight, 45, 51

Malfunction, 33, 131
Match pressure, 96, 98
Mechanism, 38, 59
Modern pentathlon, 141

N.R.A., 20, 172
N.S.R.A., 22, 172
Natural aim, 45, 50, 78, 117, 125, 136

Orthoptics, 41

Pistols, air, 71, 72, 130
　care of, 36, 37, 102
　cases, 21, 39
Police, 21

175

INDEX

Range official, 32, 33, 122, 136, 145, 154
Reaction time, 54, 95
Recoil, 59, 119, 134, 140

Safety, 26, 30, 31, 32, 34, 38, 161
Score book, 41, 115
Security, 25, 32
Sights, 41, 104
   adjustment, 65–68, 131
   alignment, 137
   mirror, 104–106
Smoking, 90
Stance, 42 et seq, 120, 124
   oblique, 42
   in line or duelling, 42, 124

Standard handgun, 141
Standard pistol (U.I.T.), 132

Team selection, 147, 151
Telescope, 39, 40, 138
Trigger, 31, 34, 38, 84, 85, 125
   mechanism, 60, 61, 101, 123
   release, 55, 56, 106, 107, 134, 137
Twitch, 47, 86

U.I.T., 22, 106, 132, 149

Vision, 53